EGYPT

CONTENTS

CHRONOLOGY

EARLY DYNASTIC PERIOD
3150-2686 B.C.

1st Dynasty
Narmer
Aha
Djer
Djet
Den
Semerkhet
Qa'a

2nd Dynasty
Hetepsekhemwy
Raneb
Nynetjer
Peribsen
Khasekhemwy

OLD KINGDOM
2686-2181 B.C.

3rd Dynasty
Sanakht
Djoser
Sekhemket
Khaba
Huni

4th Dynasty
Sneferu
Khufu
Djedefra
Khephren
Menkaure
Shepseskaf

5th Dynasty
Userkaf
Sahura
Neferirkara-Kakai
Shepsaskara
Raneferef
Nyuserra
Menkauhor
Djedkara
Unas

6th Dynasty
Teti
Pepy I
Merenra
Pepy II

FIRST INTERMEDIATE PERIOD
2181 - 2060 B.C.

7th Dynasty *(totally unknown)*

8th Dynasty *(from Memphis)*
Wadjkara
Kakara Ibi

9th and 10th Dynasties *(from Herakleopolis)*
Khety I
Merykara
Neferkara
Khety II

11th Dynasty *(Theban and contemporary with the end of the 10th Dynasty)*
Mentuhotpe I
Intef I
Intef II
Intef III

Middle Kingdom
2 060 - 1 782 B.C.

11th Dynasty
Mentuhotpe II
Mentuhotpe III
Mentuhotpe IV

12th Dynasty
Amenemhet I
Senusret I
Amenemhet II
Senwuret II
Senwuret III
Amenemhet III
Amenemhet IV
Sobekneferu

SECOND INTERMEDIATE PERIOD
1782 - 1570 B.C.

13th Dynasty *(a dynasty during which the kings, who are native Egyptians, still seem to reign over the two kingdoms of Egypt, the capital of which is in Iti-Tawi, in the oasis of el-Faiyum)*
Wegaf
Intef IV
Hor
Sebekhotpe II
Khendjer
Sebekhotpe III
Neferhotpe I
Sebekhotpe IV
Aya
Neferhotpe II

14th Dynasty *(contemporary with the end of the 13th dynasty, which ends in an obscure fashion; the 14th Dynasty only reigns over the eastern part of the Delta)*
Nehesy

15th and 16th Dynasties *(Hyksos dynasties: these kings, coming from the East, take power in Egypt and set up their capital in Avaris)*
Sharek
Yakub-Har
Khyan
Apepi I
Apepi II
Anather
Yakobaam

17th Dynasty *(Theban Dynasty, who tried to win back the land by driving out the Hyksos)*
Sebekemsaf II
Intef VII
Taa I
Taa II
Kamose

NEW KINGDOM
1570 - 1070 B. C.

18th Dynasty
Ahmose
Amenhotep I
Tuthmosis I
Tuthmosis II
Hatshepsut
Tuthmosis III
Amenhotep II
Tuthmosis IV
Amenhotep III
Amenhotep IV-Akhenaten
Smenkhkara
Tutankhamun
Ay
Horemheb

19th Dynasty
Ramesses I
Sethos I
Ramesses II
Merneptah
Amenmessu
Sethos II
Siptah
Tausret

20th Dynasty
Sethnakhte
Ramesses III
Ramesses IV-Ramesses XI

THIRD INTERMEDIATE PERIOD
1070 - 656 B. C.

21st Dynasty (*two contemporary kingdoms: the priest kings usurp the power and reign in Thebes over Upper Egypt, whereas in the Delta, Smendes proclaims himself king at the death of Ramesses XI, sets up his capital in Tanis and reigns over Lower Egypt*)

Tanis	Thebes
Smendes I	Herihor
Amenemnisu	Piankh
Psusennes I	Pinedjem I
Amenemope	Masaharta
Osorkon the Elder	Menkheperre'
Siamun	Smendes II
Psusennes II	Pinedjem II

22nd Dynasty (*Lybian dynasty, coming from Bubastis and reigning in Tanis*)
Sheshonq I
Osorkon I
Sheshonq II
Takelot I
Osorkon II
Takelot II
Sheshonq III
Pimay
Sheshonq V
Osorkon IV
Harsiesis

23rd Dynasty (*contemporary with the end of the 22nd Dynasty, the first ruling in the Delta over Lower Egypt, and the second ruling in Leontopolis over Middle Egypt*)
Pedubastis I
Sheshonq IV
Osorkon III
Takelot III
Rudamon
Iuput

24th Dynasty (*first Dynasty of Sais*)
Tefnakht
Bocchoris

25th Dynasty (*from Nubia: the kings of Napata take over the rule in Egypt*)
Piy
Shabaqo
Shabitqo
Taharqo
Tanutamani

LATE PERIOD
664 - 332 B.C.

26th Dynasty (*second Dynasty of Sais*)
Psamtek I
Nekau
Psamtek II
Apries
Ahmose
Psamtek III

27th Dynasty (*first Persian rule*)
Cambyses
Darius I
Xerxes
Artaxerxes I
Darius II
Artaxerxes II

28th Dynasty   Amyrtaios

29th Dynasty   Nepherites I
Hakor

30th Dynasty   Nectanebo I
Teos
Nectanebo II

31st Dynasty (*second Persian rule*)
Artaxerxes III
Arses
Darius III Codoman

332-323 B.C. *In 332 B.C., Alexander the Great enters into Egypt and frees the country of the Persian rule by chasing Darius III away. At his death in 323, Egypt passes under the government of one of his lieutenants, Ptolemy, who takes the title of pharaoh in 305 and founds the Ptolemaic dynasty.*

305-30 B.C. -   Ptolemaic Dynasty
Ptolemy I Soter I
Ptolemy II Philadelphus
Ptolemy III Euergetes I
Ptolemy IV Philopator
Ptolemy V Epiphanes
Ptolemy VI Philometor
Ptolemy VII Neos Philopator
Ptolemy VIII Euergetes II
Ptolemy IX Soter II
Ptolemy X Alexander I
Ptolemy XI Alexander II
Ptolemy XII Neos Dionysos
Ptolemy XIII and Cleopatra VII
Ptolemy XIV and Cleopatra VII
Cleopatra VII

30 B.C. - 395 A.D. - ROMAN EGYPT

THE COSMOGONIES
AND
THE GODS OF EGYPT

HELIOPOLITAN COSMOGONY – THE ENNEAD

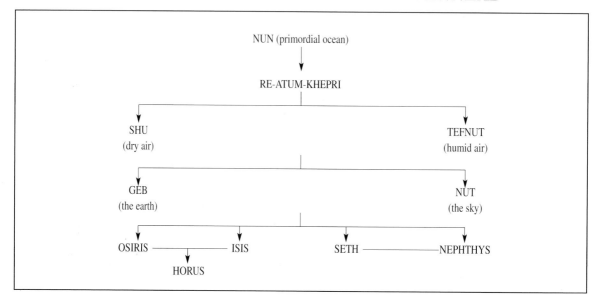

NUN (primordial ocean)

RE-ATUM-KHEPRI

SHU (dry air) — TEFNUT (humid air)

GEB (the earth) — NUT (the sky)

OSIRIS — ISIS — SETH — NEPHTHYS

HORUS

HERMOPOLITAN COSMOGONY – THE OGDOAD

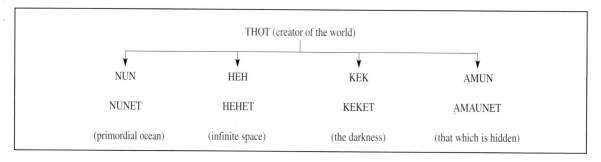

NUN	HEH	KEK	AMUN
NUNET	HEHET	KEKET	AMAUNET
(primordial ocean)	(infinite space)	(the darkness)	(that which is hidden)

THOT (creator of the world)

THE GODS OF EGYPT

AMUN: God of Thebes who became a dynastic god starting in the Middle Kingdom.

ANUKIS: A goddess of the Island of Siheil (in the First Cataract region), she formed a triad with the goddess Satis and the god Khnum.

ANUBIS: Funeral god represented as a dog or black jackal.

APIS: The sacred bull adored and worshipped in Memphis, considered a personification of the god Ptah.

ATEN: God of the sun-disk, he was worshipped as early as the Middle Kingdom and was promoted to a divinity by Amenhotep IV.

ATUM: Sun god worshipped as a creator god in Heliopolis who was assimilated with the course of the sun.

BAST: Cat goddess venerated in Bubastis in the Delta.

BES: Household genie who dispelled evil spirits and protected women in child-birth.

GEB: Divinity who personified the earth and who, with Nut, belonged to the second divine couple.

HAPI: Personification of the flooding of the Nile who guaranteed the fertility of the Egyptian soil.

HATHOR: Goddess of beauty, joy, and of love represented as a cow or as a woman with a headdress of horns surrounding the sun-disk. She was an assimilation of numerous local goddesses and was one of the most popular deities of the Egyptian pantheon.

HEQUET: The frog-headed goddess of Antinoopolis, she was often associated with the god Khnum through the system of divine births.

HORAKHTY (OR HARMAKHIS): "Horus of the Horizon"; a form of the sun god worshipped in Heliopolis.

HORUS: Son of Isis and Osiris represented in the form of a falcon. He is the most important dynastic god and the supreme god of celestial spaces. However, the Egyptians worshipped many divinities under the name Horus.

ISIS: One of the most popular Egyptian goddesses, she was distinguished by her strong personality. Sister and wife of Osiris, mother of Horus.

KHEPRI: God worshipped in Heliopolis, represented by a scarab-beetle. He symbolised the sun that was unfailingly reborn every morning.

KHNUM: Worshipped at Elephantine and at Esna, this ram-headed god was thought to have moulded man on a potter's wheel.

KHONS: The moon god with the head of a falcon, honored in Thebes as the son of Amun and Mut.

MAAT: Goddess of universal order, justice, and truth, often symbolized by an ostrich feather.

MIN: God of fertility, often associated with Amun, represented as an ithyphallic god.

MNEVIS: Name of the sacred bull of Heliopolis, and an incarnation of Re', the sun god.

MENTU: God of war with the head of a falcon worshipped at Hermonthis.

MUT: Vulture goddess of Thebes associated with Amun and with her son, the god Khons.

NEFERTUM: Personification of the primordial lotus, from which the sun emerged. Son of Ptah and Sakhmet.

NEITH: The war goddess of Sais in the Delta.

NEKHBET: Vulture goddess of El-Kab, tutelary deity of Upper Egypt.

NEPHTHYS: Sister of Isis and Osiris, sister and wife of Seth, who plays a secondary role in the cult of the dead.

NUN: The primordial ocean. In the Heliopolitan cosmology, she is responsible for the creation of the world.

NUT: Female divinity personifying the celestial vault and belonging to the second divine couple along with Geb.

ONURIS: God of the city of This wearing a feather headdress and brandishing a harpoon.

OSIRIS: God of vegetation, but above all god of the dead after having been resurrected by his sister and wife, Isis, with whom he posthumously conceived a child, Horus.

PAKHET: Goddess with the head of a lioness worshipped in Middle Egypt.

PTAH: Dynastic god of Memphis in the Old Kingdom, in Memphite theology considered to be the creator of the world and the inventor of crafts.

RE': The supreme sun god, one of the most celebrated gods of the Egyptian pantheon, even though his cult originated in Heliopolis.

SATIS: Patron goddess of the First Cataract, she forms a triad with the god Khnum and the goddess Anukis.

SESHAT: Patron goddess, with Thot, of writing and the sciences.

SEKHMET: Symbolic of destructive power, she is represented with a head of a lioness. Wife of Ptah and mother of Nefertum.

SELKIS: Goddess whose head was adorned with the image of a scorpion. With Isis, Nephthys, and Neith, protectress of the dead.

SERAPIS: The Greek name of Apis, the sacred bull of Memphis.

SETH: God associated with evil due to his role in the assassination of Osiris. Husband and brother of Nephthys, brother of Isis and Osiris. Fought with Horus over Osiris legacy.

SHU: God of air and space belonging to the first divine couple, along with Tefnut.

SOBK: The crocodile-god, especially adored in the Fayum, and at Kom Ombo and Gebelein.

SOKARIS: God who resided at the border of the eastern desert. Considered along with Ptah and Osiris as a funerary god.

SOPDU: Falcon-god of the eastern Delta.

TEFNUT: The goddess of moisture belonging, with Shu, to the first divine couple.

THOT: Moon god in the form of an ibis or a baboon, especially honored at Hermopolis. Patron of calculation, sciences, and letters and scribes. He participated in the weighing of souls during the judgment of the deceased.

THOERIS: Hippopotamus-goddess, protective of mothers and children.

WADJET: The cobra goddess of Buto, tutelary goddess of Lower Egypt.

THE BIRTH OF EGYPT

Egypt is "a gift of the Nile." This definition, given by the Greek historian Herodotus who travelled through the country in 450 BC, is the most famous and remains accurate to this day.

The Aswan Dam, which regulates the flow of water, was constructed with the sole purpose of extricating Egypt from its eternal dependence on the Nile and its capricious floods.

Like a long oasis between two deserts, Egypt stretches for a thousand miles along the Nile Valley, from the Second Cataract in Nubia to the Mediterranean, where the river flows into a vast delta with six branches.

Life in Ancient Egypt was determined by the rhythm of the annual flooding of the Nile. Each year around the 15th of June in Aswan, and then six to twelve days later in Memphis, the tropical rains that soaked the Abyssinia highlands and the thawing African snows swelled the river. The rising waters carried with them black alluvial soil. When the river finally overflowed, it drenched and fertilized the earth. After the water retreated, all that was left was to work the land, now easier because the earth was soft and humid. The Egyptians saw their country as synonymous with this black earth. They often called it "Kemet," which means "Black Land," and contrasted it to "Desheret," the "Red Land" of the desert.

The beginning of the flood coincided with the rising of the star Sothis, or Sopdet, and which we call Sirius. The Egyptians fixed this date as the beginning of their year. The flood determined three seasons: "Akhet," the inundation season, lasting from June to October; "Peret," the growing season, from November to February; and "Shomu," the harvest season, from March to June.

Depending on the flood, the population experienced either prosperity or drought. A too-abundant flood or an insufficient one brought with it a year of "lean cows." The people prayed to the god Hapi to give Egypt an adequate flood. The pharaoh himself led the procession in Gebel Silsileh.

Hapi symbolized the spirit of the Nile. He was represented as an androgynous being, with a bare chest and pendulous breasts, and he wore a crown of papyrus. The Nile itself was called "Iteru," which meant simply "river." This became Yeor, the name of the Delta. "Na-Yeor," the plural of Yeor, is perhaps the origin of the Greek term, "Neilos," the Nile.

The Nile was the main source of life, because it hardly ever rains in Upper Egypt. A very different climate prevailed during the Palaeolithic age and at the outset of the Neolithic age. The North African regions and the Eastern Mediterranean were humid, wooded, and grassy.

Climatic changes caused a progressive drying up and desertification of this land, forcing the Nomads toward the Nile Valley, lush with tropical flora and fauna. A population of diverse cultures, among them Mediterraneans, Semites, Berbers, and Blacks, settled along the marshlands and ponds that formed the Nile Valley. There, thickets of roses and papyrus provided shelter to hippopotami and crocodiles. The tribes stopped their wanderings and settled in the Valley. They drained and irrigated the land and domesticated the areas inundated by the Nile's annual flooding. Villages sprang up throughout the Valley. The people lived from hunting, fishing, and cultivating crops. The exploitation of the Nile Valley intensified, and little by little the villages grouped into provinces that prefigured the pharaonic nomes (administrative provinces).

Osiris, Anubis, and Horus
Tomb walls from the New Kingdom are covered with representations and names of gods and spirits. These illustrate text from the Book of the Dead. *Here, Osiris, god of the dead; Anubis, god of funeral rites; and Horus, god of the dynasty, help the pharaoh Haremhab take the final steps and ascend to the afterworld.*

The King Khasekhemwy

As of the eleventh Dynasty, schist statues as remarkable as this one of Khasekhemwy appeared in Hieraconpolis. Wearing the white crown of Upper Egypt, the king is wrapped in the long cloak of the Sed festival. He is seated in a posture that became traditional in Egypt. The base of his throne depicts enemies vanquished by the pharaoh.

Vestiges of diverse prehistoric cultures have been found, such as the Badarian culture (around 5000 BC), the Amratian culture (around 4000 BC) and the Gerzean culture (around 3500 BC). The prehistoric peoples of the Nile believed in the afterlife. Tombs full of vases and other utensils surrounding the deceased have been unearthed. The corpse was always very well-preserved thanks to hot desert sands that helped keep the tissues dry.

Starting in the fourth millennium BC, the Egyptians had contacts and commercial exchanges with Mesopotamia, another important center of civilization, and Crete. The provinces regrouped to form two kingdoms. The kingdom of Lower Egypt to the north had Wadjet, the cobra goddess of Buto, located in the Delta, as its tutelary goddess. The kingdom of Upper Egypt to the south was under the protection of the vulture goddess Nekhbet, who was honored in El-Kab, near Hieraconpolis. Some historians believe that this division was based more on a natural division of the country rather than on bona fide politically organized kingdoms.

Lower Egypt, with its Mediterranean climate, was a vast stretch of streams, river branches, marshlands, prairies, gardens, and vineyards. It boasted a cosmopolitan population. It seems that Lower Egyptian culture was more developed than that of Upper Egypt, which was trapped between two desert cliffs, the Libyan on the west and the Arabian on the east.

Near the end of the Gerzean period, from 3300 BC to about 3200 BC, it seems that the sovereigns of the north and the south fought for supremacy over Egypt.

It was around 3200 BC that Pharaonic Egypt was born. The birth of a united kingdom coincided with the first evidence of writing.

The union of the north and south was blessed by the protection of Horus, the falcon god of Hieraconpolis, located in Upper Egypt, and was the work of one of the southern sovereigns.

The identity of this unifying pharaoh has been the subject of fierce debate. Although opinion is divided, many believe he was Narmer, who figures on a schist slab. This slab is called the Narmer Plate and is one of the first documents of writing.

The king wears the red crown of Lower Egypt on one side of the plate, and the white crown of

THE ROSETTA STONE

Upper Egypt on the other. The plate commemorates a victory, and the king is depicted as an incarnation of the god Horus.

It is generally believed that Narmer and the legendary Menes, Memphis founder whom the Egyptians told Herodotus was the first king of Egypt, were one and the same.

That notwithstanding, it appears that a certain Scorpion King who figures in a mace head found in Hieraconpolis and dating from around 3225 BC may have actually unified Egypt before Narmer.

The first and second dynasties reigned from about 3200 to 2780 BC. This period is called Thinite, on account of the then capital, This (also Thinis), near Abydos in Upper Egypt. We know little about this era.

We have but very incomplete sources. A list of kings, divided into dynasties, has survived. It was penned by the High Priest Manethon, who wrote a multivolume history of Egypt in Greek under Ptolemy Philadelphus. Unfortunately, this work was lost in the burning of the library of Alexandria, but some fragments came to us indirectly, through the writings of library users in the third and fourth centuries AD. Two other sources take up Manethon's cataloguing: the *Royal Canon of Turin* establishes a list of all the pharaohs with the duration of their reign and their capitals; and the *Palermo Stone* covers the first five dynasties and the significant happenings of some of the reigns.

The necropolis at Abydos attests to This supremacy. Sepultures with stelae bearing the precise names of the pharaohs of the first two dynasties were found in Abydos.

All the same, Memphis – which, legend holds, was founded by Menes, the first pharaoh – became quite important, on account of its location on the tip of the Delta. Numerous tombs attributed to high functionaries of the first and second dynasties were found at Sakkarah, Memphis's necropolis. From Memphis, these dignitaries could oversee all the domains of Lower Egypt.

The Rosetta Stone

Thanks to the discovery of the Rosetta Stone by an officer in Napoleon's army in 1799, Champollion was able to unlock the key to the hieroglyphs in 1822. The stele bears a decree by Ptolemy Epiphanes, transcribed in hieroglyphs, demotic, and Greek. The comparison of these three texts led to the progressive deciphering of the Egyptian signs.

The Tomb
of Amenhotep II

There are six pillars in the sarcophagus room of Amenhotep II's tomb in the Valley of the Kings. On each of their sides, a god is depicted holding the ankh, symbolic of the breath of life, under the king's nose. The scenes total 24 and are very representative of the Egyptian pantheon. Depicted here are Osiris, wearing his three attributes (the whip, the was scepter, and the heqa cross), and the goddess Hathor, wearing a headdress of two cow horns encircling the solar disk.

Memphis was one of the most important religious centers of its time. The primary cult was that of the god Ptah, "he who has formed all the gods, men, and animals, he who has created all lands." The priests at Memphis developed one of the three great cosmogonies of Egypt.

According to the Memphite theology (the more abstract of the three), through his thought Ptah brought eight gods into existence – his hypostases, who together with him constituted the creative Ennead.

The first four of these gods are Tatjenen, the earth born of the primordial ocean; Nun and Nunet, the male and female principles of this ocean; and Atum, the sun. It is generally believed that the other four gods were Horus, "Ptah's intelligence"; Thot, "Ptah's will"; a serpent-god; and Nefertum, the lotus-god.

In the Heliopolis cosmogony, it was the sun god Re'-Atum-Khepri who emerged from Nun, the primordial ocean, to engender, through either masturbation or expectoration, the first divine couple, Shu (the air) and Tefnut (humidity). This couple conceived the god Geb (the earth) and the goddess Nut (the sky), who in turn gave birth to Osiris and Iris, Seth and Nephthys.

In the third system, from Hermopolis, Thot simply supplanted the Ogdoad who had created light. The Ogdoad consisted of four couples shaped as frogs and serpents: Nun and Nunet, the primordial ocean; Heh and Hehet, the infinite space; Kek and Keket, the darkness; Amun and Amaunet, that which is hidden.

It is thought that the name "Egypt" comes from Memphis. The Egyptians themselves called their country "Kemet", "the BlackLand", or else "Ta-Meri," the beloved land. It was also called "Ta-Nutri," the land of the gods, or "the Two Lands," underlining the north/south duality.

The Greek term "Aegyptos," in use since the Homeric Age, may have been derived from a corruption of "Ha-Kah-Ptah," "the castle of Ptah's Ka," which is the name of the great temple of Ptah in Memphis.

We know almost nothing of the political events that marked the first two dynasties. The passage from the first to the second was certainly violent. Succession was already a source of conflict. Under the second dynasty, the country was divided into two kingdoms, with their capitals at Memphis and This. King Khasekhemwy put an end to the battles.

Writing first appeared around 3200 BC, with the union of North and South under the authority of a single king. During the Thinite period, it showed considerable progress.

At first purely ideographic (that is, composed of drawings designating the actual drawn object), writing became syllabic: the signs became phonograms transcribing sounds, like the rebus. Later, certain signs became letters, but vowels were not transcribed.

During the classical era, hieroglyphs numbered seven hundred; during the decadence, two thousand.

On account of this astounding complexity, the language of ancient Egypt remained inaccessible to us for a long time. In Egypt, the use of hieroglyphs disappeared around the fourth century AD.

In 1799, an officer in Napoleon's army discovered the famous "Rosetta Stone," which bears inscriptions in three languages: hieroglyphic, demotic (cursive Egyptian writing), and Greek.

In 1822, Champollion understood that the hieroglyphic language was at once ideographic and syllabic, and he succeeded in deciphering the names "Cleopatra" and "Ptolemy," surrounded by a cartouche like all royal names in Egyptian. This was the beginning of a long series of discoveries. Mysterious Egypt slowly began to yield its secrets to us.

The development of writing paralleled the growth of economy and commerce. During the Thinite Period, Egypt was a state centralised around royal power. A potent administration oversaw the control of arable lands, granaries, the production of wine and oils, the collection of taxes, and the running of the treasury. The army attended to the security of the frontiers. Administrative houses similar to ministries (like the House of Water that controlled the Nile, and the White House that managed the finances) were headed by high functionaries named by the king. He also named the governors of the provinces (or "nomes"). At the top of the hierarchy, the king was surrounded by the Council of Ten, who assisted him.

Besides being the chief of the army and of diplomacy, the pharaoh (a later term, derived from "per-aa," which meant great house or palace), was the chief of clergy. In theory, the privilege of celebrating the cult of the gods was his alone.

Page 20:
The Narmer Palette

This schist palette, engraved with King Narmer's name, symbolizes the unification of Egypt around 3200 BC. Narmer, protected by the goddess Hathor and wearing the white crown of Upper Egypt, wields his mace over the head of an inhabitant of the marshes. From an artistic point of view, this is a primordial work, as it announces the various stylistic canons that endured throughout Egyptian history.

In practice he was often obliged to delegate his function to the priest of each temple. The Egyptian monarchy was sacred, destined to perpetuate upon the earth the divine order, "ma'at," that reflected the golden age's perfection. The pharaoh, incarnation of "ma'at," had the duty of keeping chaos at bay, thereby maintaining the cosmic and social order and ensuring the permanence of divine effort. He was a model to his subjects and the master of the people, of the land, and of possessions. Divine utterance, "Hu," and divine perception, "Sia," inspired him.

The king transmitted his power and his functions to his oldest son or brother or, in their absence, to a woman. Nitokris, Hatshepsut, and Tausret were famous women pharaohs.

The ceremony of enthronement of the new pharaoh reproduced the rites of the mythical founding of the unified state by Menes. The ceremony of the jubilee, or Sed festival, celebrated after thirty years' reign, emulated this ritual. Events were dated in relationship with each reign. Moreover, the old lunar calendar was replaced by a solar one of twelve months of thirty days, with the addition of five extra feast days.

Representations of the pharaoh always depicted him of equal size to the gods. As king, he was bound by complex rituals. He bore the pshent, or double crown, consisting of the white crown of Upper Egypt and the red crown of Lower Egypt; the scepter and false beard; an animal tail; and the uraeus, a magical insignia in the shape of a snake that was worn over the crown and called "the Eye of Re'."

Little by little, an elaborate protocol evolved around the name of the king, including the designations "His Majesty," "Life, Health, Strength," and five royal names, of which the last two were enclosed by the cartouche, symbol of the magic circle.

From early on in its history Pharaonic Egypt thus established political, cultural, and religious structures that it fought to perpetuate, believing these structures to be the earthly manifestation of divine order.

The uraeus

The cobra wearing the crown of Lower Egypt represents Wadjet, the protector goddess of the North.

THE OLD KINGDOM

The pyramid builders

Traditionally, the third Dynasty inaugurates the Old Kingdom. It started around 2780 BC with Pharaoh Nebka. Apparently, the transition from the second to the third dynasties was relatively smooth.

The pharaohs of the third dynasty established their capital in Memphis. It was the beginning of a new era of splendor and prosperity that saw the founding of classical Egyptian culture.

Already an important religious center during the Thinite period, Memphis became a political, cultural, and commercial center of the first order. The pharaohs crowned themselves in Memphis, where they built their official residences. Located south of the Delta, where branches of the Nile tangled with canals, Memphis became a flourishing port. Crafts and metalwork developed during this period.

Djoser, the second king of the third dynasty, was the first pharaoh to control the Sinai Peninsula and its turquoise and copper mines.

In Memphis, the god Ptah was venerated. Early on, Ptah was associated with Apis, the sacred bull who was considered an incarnation of the god. Later, the lioness-goddess Sekhmet came to dwell in Memphis as Ptahs' wife and mother of Nefertum, the lotus-god.

In the capital, Sokaris, the god of the necropolis who was later absorbed into Osiris, and Hathor were also celebrated.

Djoser, Imhotep, and Saqqara

Stone architecture was born under King Djoser "the magnificent." Under the Thinite dynasties, important buildings such as palaces, temples, and the mastabas of Saqqara and Abydos were made of unbaked mud bricks and of wood imported from Lebanon. These materials had replaced the bulrush, papyrus, and clay-covered reeds of the archaic era.

From the beginning of the Old Kingdom, stone was used for parts of certain buildings, but the first to build entirely in stone was Pharaoh Djosers' architect, Imhotep. Stone architecture arose from the desire to build "eternal homes", first for kings, then for high functionaries. Djoser was the first pharaoh to bear the title of Golden Horus: the flesh of the pharaohs is golden like that of the deities. For such a king, an eternal home was a necessity of his eternal life.

The task of transforming (with stone, a durable material) the palace of the living king into a grand palace for the deceased king fell upon Imhotep, a brilliant architect. He created the first royal tomb in the shape of a pyramid.

The Egyptian people recognized Imhoteps' greatness. Initially artisan and priest at Heliopolis, subsequently Djosers' chancellor, Imhotep was renowned as architect, scribe, astronomer, and physician, and, during a later period, was even venerated as a healing god and a patron of scribes.

Imhotep built his greatest opus on the Saqqara plateau at the edge of the desert near Memphis.

This immense funerary complex in white limestone includes: the first Egyptian step pyramid, conceived as a superposition of six mastabas of diminishing dimensions above a set of underground funerary chambers and galleries; a mastaba functioning as a second tomb, with an underground, pink granite funerary chamber without a sarcophagus; rows of chapels, sanctuaries, and houses around a vast court; a colonnaded entrance; and a wall surrounding the entire complex with fourteen false doors.

The Giza Sphinx

Facing the rising sun, the Giza Sphinx represents a crouching lion with a human head whose face resembles that of King Chephren. Considered a symbol of the god Harmakhis, the "Horus of the Horizon," it was meant to guard the royal necropolis. Admired even in ancient times by travellers, the majestic Sphinx still astounds those who see it.

The Memphis Sphinx

Discovered in 1912 at Mit Rahina at the site of ancient Memphis, this gigantic sphinx now measures 4 metres (13 ft.) high and 8 metres (26 ft.) long. It must have belonged to the temple of Ptah, Memphis protector god. Long attributed to Ramesses II, its stylistic characteristics appear more typical of the beginning of the 18th dynasty.

Its architecture is essentially symbolic. The majority of the buildings in the complex were meant to play a magical role. Artificial decorative elements abound: false doors and windows, false beams, simulated fences, stone curtains and mural panels imitating the reed wallpaper found in homes and decorated with blue tiles. Inside the chambers, a variety of objects were found: numerous vases in stone, alabaster, and rock crystal; statues depicting the king; bas-reliefs; stone crockery including cups, bowls, and plates; and the friezes of djed pillars symbolizing the kings' stability.

The architecture of the step pyramid, formed of mastabas piled in an ascending order, reflects the growing importance of the solar theology of Heliopolis, where Imhotep was high priest.

The steps are the symbolic ladder that allows the kings' heavenly ascension. In effect, it was the kings' privilege to have a solar destiny following his death. The deceased sovereign climbed to heaven to rejoin Re – or, according to other formulations, he took flight in the form of a falcon or a scarab-beetle. In the skies, he was received triumphantly by the sun god.

The sarcophagus chamber – the true tomb of the king meant to house his mummy – was cut into the stone under the pyramid. Mummification preserved his body from destruction.

At first, only the kings and persons of royal blood were embalmed.

The embalming technique was very thorough; the body was entirely emptied, cleaned, and stuffed with aromatic spices. The viscera, cleaned with palm wine and aromatic spices, were put aside in special vases called canopic jars. Then the body was plunged into a vat full of natron, where it stayed for seventy days.

Once the desiccation was achieved, the embalmers washed the body with perfumed oils and swathed it with resin-soaked linen strips. All these procedures were accompanied by prayers and litanies recited by priests, who sometimes wore the masks of Anubis, the jackal-god and guardian of the necropolis. In later times, mummification was extended to everyone. Many different classes of embalming were available, and the costs varied accordingly.

The sarcophagus chamber was surrounded by funerary halls full of offerings. A little room, the serdab, contained the statue of Djoser, the putative incarnation of the pharaohs' "ka", a kind of spiritual double or vital force that remained lively after death.

The Egyptians called the deceased "he who has passed into his "ka" or he who has rejoined his "akh" (the principle of a celestial spirit). The "ka" of the deceased remained inside the tomb, walking about the funerary halls and tasting the gathered offerings. The soul, or "ba," of the deceased left his body in the form of a bird and roamed.

The funerary complex of Djoser was the wonder of its era. It was restored in modern times by Jean-Philippe Lauer.

Djoser' successors in the third Dynasty continued with the style of the step pyramid. King Sekhemket undertook the construction of a vast funerary complex in Saqqara, but he died before work was completed, and the complex was never finished.

Sneferu

King Sneferu founded the fourth Dynasty around 2720 BC. Today the fourth dynasty is seen first and foremost as the dynasty of grand pyramid builders. Sneferu was a very active sovereign in an Egypt that was undergoing tremendous development. During his reign, all the state-run systems of production were under the strictest control. Sneferu created inventories for livestock; exploited the mines in the Sinai more efficiently than ever before; and organised an expedition to Lebanon to bring back timber wood of cedar and pine. Security on the Nubian and Libyan fronts was guaranteed by regular military operations.

Sneferu instituted the office of vizier. This was an administrator appointed in the name of the king and reporting directly to the nomarchs. He was head of the army, of justice, and of agriculture. He was given the kings' full confidence.

Sneferu was a popular pharaoh and was called the "Good King." He was the object of local cults, in the Sinai and in Dahshur, as well as the subject of many stories and legends.

One of these, the *Tale of the Rowing Maidens*, has come down to us through a manuscript known as the *Westcar Papyrus*. This document contains a series of wonderful stories which supposedly happened during the fourth dynasty. Another of these stories, called *A Prophetic Tale*, was very famous in Egypt. It was studied and copied in schools as a classical work during the 18th and 19th dynasties.

The unfinished step pyramid of Meidum is attributed to Sneferu. It is believed, however, that the pyramid was actually dedicated to his predecessor, Huni, the last king of the third Dynasty. It was in one of the tombs near this pyramid that the archaeologist Mariette found the famous statues of Prince Rahotep and his wife Nofret, their colors still bright and their eyes full of life.

At Dahshur, King Sneferu built two pyramids with triangular sides. One, located in the south, is called the "Bent Pyramid" due to the abrupt change of its angle about midway. The north pyramid, with its regular and gentle slope, is the first "true" Egyptian pyramid.

Chephren in Giza

Several monuments from Chephrens' funerary complex have survived in Giza: the pyramid, with its casing still intact at the summit; the road that leads to the granite temple that is still in place; and finally the Sphinx, which guards the entire necropolis.

Djosers' pyramid in Saqqara

Djosers' funerary complex remains the earliest example of stone architecture in Egypt. Built by Imhotep, the step pyramid is a result of three successive phases of construction: a mastaba, a sort of rectangular superstructure above the cave; then a pyramid with four steps; and finally a permanent, six-stepped pyramid.

The Pyramid of Meidum

Begun by Huni and finished by Sneferu, his successor, the pyramid in Meidum offers a singular aspect: it represents a mid-point between the step pyramid in Saqqara and the first true pyramid in Dahshur. The top two levels, above a mastaba, seem to have been covered by a uniform limestone casing that was destroyed in the New Kingdom.

The Bent Pyramid

The complex at Dahshur includes this surprising stone pyramid, called the "Bent Pyramid" because of its shape. It is characterized by an abrupt change in inclination about mid-height. Built for Sneferu, it measures 97 metres (318 feet) high. Archaeologists still differ on the reasons for this double inclination, which seems to have been determined sometime during the construction.

The Red Pyramid of Dahshur

Erected at Dahsur for Sneferu, the Red Pyramid is the earliest known example in Egypt of a royal funerary monument constructed as a perfect pyramid. Not as tall as the pyramids of Cheops and Chephren in Giza, it measures 104 metres (341 feet) high. It seems more earthbound, however, than the latter pyramids, because its base is proportionately wider.

The Pyramids of Giza

Besides the structures built by Cheops, the necropolis at Giza also contains a fairly complete funerary complex dedicated to Chephren, which includes Chephrens' pyramid, pictured here in the background. Also in Giza is Mykerinos' pyramid, accompanied by its three smaller satellite pyramids whose purpose still remains an enigma.

The Cheops Pyramid

Of the seven wonders of the ancient world, the pyramid of Cheops is the only one to have survived through the centuries. Known as Akhet Khufu ("Cheops is luminous"), it was a pure embodiment of the Egyptians' architectural genius. According to Herodotus, the construction required 100,000 workers who worked for thirty years to construct the pyramid.

The Giza Pyramids

The three massive pyramids erected on the Giza plateau at the threshold of the western desert (realm of the dead and the setting sun) bear witness to a veritable golden age for Egypt, a time when the country was rich and powerful.

From time immemorial, travellers have been fascinated by these gigantic stone triangles. Originally, their facades were covered in a layer of smooth white limestone. Their pyramidions, pointing heavenward and covered in fine gold, symbolized petrified sun rays, a means of communication between earth and heaven which the deceased kings travelled in order to rejoin the sun god Re'.

Since Antiquity, various legends have sprouted around these grand, strange buildings and the kings who erected them. Herodotus claimed the pharaohs were accursed and that the Egyptians detested them. He let himself be persuaded that Cheops sold his daughter into prostitution so as to obtain the large amounts of money needed to build his pyramid. Cheops and Chephren, it was claimed, closed the temples, forbade sacrifices, and oppressed the populace, forcing thousands of people to work relentlessly – and in the worst possible conditions – in order to erect their pyramids.

Later, the Arabs imagined that these monuments were granaries, stocking surplus harvest as provision for years of famine.

Even today, various esoteric traditions see the Great Pyramid as a place of initiation, where the mysteries might have been celebrated; or as an astronomical observatory containing within the secret of its proportions geometric relationships and astronomical measurements that were known only to the initiated and the sages of the time.

Seductive as these theories may be for lovers of the esoteric, the pyramids' symbolic meaning, as revealed to us in the translation of the *Pyramid Texts*, written in stone by the fifth dynasty pharaoh, Unas, is more admirable still.

These edifices are the collective accomplishment of a nation moved by faith, similar to what motivated the builders of cathedrals in the Middle Ages. The people who erected them, stone by stone, with techniques that seem rudimentary to us, gathered their energies to build a ladder towards heaven.

By contributing to the glorious destiny of their king, the people linked themselves to his solar transformation, hoping that they would be drawn along into a collective, celestial afterlife. The pyramids bear witness to an ideal connected with the growth of Heliopolis.

The Great Pyramid, built by Cheops, son of Sneferu, was one of the seven wonders of the ancient world, and the only one that still exists today. Its construction was directed by Hemon, a brilliant architect and engineer who was Cheops' cousin and vizier.

The building, like the other Giza pyramids, is made of large blocks (measuring more than one cubic metre (11sq.ft.) each) cut from local limestone; it consists of two and a half million blocks. It was originally covered with a casing of finer white limestone from the quarry at Tura, on the opposite river bank. This casing was removed in the Middle Ages and used as construction material for Cairos' monuments.

Known to the Egyptians as Akhet Khufu, "Cheops' Horizon," the Great Pyramid was 146 meterss (479 ft.) high including its top; today its height is 137 metres. (449 ft.) At its base, each side measured 230 metres (754 ft.) including the casing; today this measurement is 227 metres (745 ft.). Such a large number of perfectly polished and assembled blocks, erected to such a height, presupposes flawless organization of labor and a total mastery of the technical means employed.

Modern historians, archaeologists, and engineers have proposed many hypotheses about these puzzling techniques.

Today it is thought that four ramps of mud brick and clay were constructed starting at the corners of the pyramids' square base. These then grew higher at the same time as the layers of limestone. On three of these ramps, workers hoisted the stone blocks on wooden sleds pulled by men or animals; the fourth ramp was used to return the empty sleds. The layers were thus put into place, and, once the top was finished, the casing was applied from the top downwards, and the ramps were dismantled in turn.

Today one enters the Cheops pyramid by an opening that pillagers dug fifteen metres below the rocky plateau; the old entrance is now blocked.

King Chephren

The majesty exuded by this diorite statue of King Chephren ranks it as one of the most significant masterpieces of Egyptian sculpture from the Old Kingdom. The King is seated on a finely-crafted throne, its legs decorated with the figures of lions. He is wearing the royal nemes headdress, which is made of three sections. In his right hand, he holds a piece of fabric while his left hand rests on his knee.

After entering, one follows a narrow passage that descends towards an underground funerary chamber. Quickly one arrives at a fork rising back upwards and passes through the great gallery that leads to the funerary chamber called the kings' chamber, where an empty granite sarcophagus was found; the royal mummy was probably destroyed.

In the antechamber there were granite portcullis (or sliding doors) that, after the inhumation, were meant to be closed, thereby permanently sealing the funerary chamber, but they have failed to protect against pillagers. A little lower, another funerary chamber had been fitted out; it is incorrectly called the queens' chamber.

In former times the pyramid was flanked with a funerary temple, connected by a roadway to a second temple situated at the edge of the flood waters. Next to the southern and eastern faces of the pyramid, five immense moats meant to contain boats have been restored. A single one of these boats has been recreated and reassembled. Made of cedar and 48 metres (157 ft.) in length, it contains a cabin with a canopy supported by papyrus-shaped columns. The five boats may have been meant for the deceased king as he followed the sun in his navigation towards the hereafter.

In fact, we know that the god Re' traversed the sky from east to west in his boat during the day, then descended to the "lower sky," the Amduat, realm of the dead, where he travelled during the night from west to east, before being reborn at dawn for the start of a new cycle.

Another funerary chamber – probably a second tomb for Queen Hetepheres, Sneferus' wife and Cheops' mother – was found in a secret well in the neighborhood of the Great Pyramid. This burial place contained various treasures for the queens' use during her stay in the hereafter: vases in gold and alabaster, a bed, two chairs and a canopy covered in fine gold, and a carrying chair panelled in ebony and inlaid with gold hieroglyphs.

About Cheops himself we know almost nothing, outside of legend. The *Westcar Papyrus* opens with him. At the beginning of this collection of tales, a bored Cheops asks his son, the prince, to entertain him with stories. Prince Baufre then regales him with the charming *Tale of the Rowing Maidens*, featuring King Sneferu.

Cheops' Pyramid

Each side measures 227 metres (745 ft) at the base. Its height is 137 metres (449 ft.). It has 2,300,000 stone blocks. These numbers show the immensity of Cheops' pyramid in Giza, the largest in Egypt. Today it is hard to explain how the pyramid was erected, but apparently a system of swinging ramps helped workers hoist the blocks all the way to the summit.

The pyramid of Cheops' son, Chephren, may appear more imposing than his fathers', as it rests on a higher point of the rocky plateau. Yet it is smaller. Its height today is 136 metres (446 ft.), and the side of its base measures 210 metres (689 ft.). The casing on its summit is very well preserved. Inside the funerary room, a broken sarcophagus missing its royal mummy was discovered.

The foundations of Chephrens' funerary temple and part of the roadway that leads to the lower temple are visible. Chephrens' lower temple is the best preserved of the Giza complex. It is made of pink granite. A beautiful T-shaped hall contains pink-granite pillars. In the niches between the pillars, twenty-three statues of the king in green diorite, grey schist, and alabaster were once housed.

The famous Sphinx rests next to Chephrens' lower temple. Chephrens' haughty head and the body of a seated lion rise up from the desert sands. The head is adorned with the nemes, the pharaohs' headdress. The nose was originally decorated with the uraeus, the cobra symbolizing "the Eye of Re'," but the nose and beard were destroyed by a Mameluk sultans' cannonballs.

The Sphinx is 73 metres (240 ft.) long, and the head 4,15 metres (14 ft.) high. The Sphinx was born of a rocky spur. The architects working on Chephrens'

The Granite Temple

Called the Granite Temple on account of the material from which it was built, it is in fact the valley temple belonging to Chephrens' pyramid. At one time it was located on the bank of the Nile. After the sarcophagus of the deceased king crossed the river, it was welcomed by the temple. The T-shaped temple contains many monolithic pillars of pink granite.

pyramid noticed a strangely shaped rock near the valley temple. They gave form to this mass of limestone and created the majestic guardian in the image of King Chephren or of the god Re'-Harakhti or Harakhti, Re'-Horus of the Horizon.

Between the Sphinxs' paws, a stele erected by Thutmose IV commemorates a legendary event. While hunting on the Giza plateau, Prince Thutmose (who lived during the 15th century BC) fell asleep under the shade of the rocky head, which at the time was the only visible part of the Sphinx; the rest was covered in sand. The Sphinx came to him in a dream, predicting that one day he would be king of Egypt and asking him to free it of the sands that covered it.

When he ascended to the throne, Thutmose IV remembered the Sphinxs' prediction and cleared the sands away. Later, the Sphinx was once again submerged in sand, until the archaeologist Maspero definitively saved it from oblivion in 1886.

The pyramid built by Mykerinos, Chephrens' son, is much smaller than those of his predecessors. Today it is 62 metres (203 ft.) high, and at its base its side measures 108 metres (354 ft.).

In Mykerinos' funerary temple, some very beautiful groups were discovered. These show the king flanked by the queen (or a goddess) on one side, and the personification of a nome (or province) on the other.

Many legends exist about Mykerinos. Herodotus claimed that Fate set upon this king, despite his being just and popular. Very distressed by the death of his only daughter, he had her buried inside a gold-covered statue in the shape of a cow.

Herodotus also tells us another version, in which Mykerinos, in love with his daughter, took her by force. She killed herself in despair, and the king then had her buried in the cow-shaped coffin.

Mykerinos' Triad

In Mykerinos' valley in Giza, several triads in green schist were found. These represent the king flanked by the goddess Hathor to his right and another goddess to his left. Here we see the protector goddess of the Egyptian Cynopolite nome. These sculptures are among the masterpieces of the Old Kingdom.

The sons of Re'

The fifth dynasty witnessed the ascent of Heliopolis' omnipotence and of its god Re'. The pharaoh, formerly an incarnate god, became "the son of Re'." This honorific now began to appear systematically in the royal titulary.

During this period, Heliopolis (the sun city, in Greek, and called "On" in Egyptian) supplanted Memphis as the religious capital. The solar cosmogony, with the god Re' at its center, elaborated by the Heliopolitan priests became all-powerful. The myths of creation abounded. The sun god now took multiple forms. In the morning, he was associated with the scarab-beetle symbolizing the rising sun, and was called Khepri, after the verb "kheper," to come into existence, to be born. At noon he was Re', in all his glory. In the evening he was Atum, the setting sun, depicted as an old man. Atum was the name of the archaic sun god of Heliopolis. The solar disk itself, casting down its beneficial rays upon men, was worshipped under the name of Aten. Re' also took the form of the falcon Horus, the bird that moved in the infinity of celestial space, and was assimilated under the name of Re'-Horakhry, represented as a falcon bearing the solar disk as a headdress. The sun

Hathor and Sahure

Sahure was the second king of the fifth dynasty. Of his funerary complex in Abusir, there remains unfortunately only the collapsed pyramid and a few vestiges of the funerary temple. Their exceptional quality allows one to imagine what they must have been once upon a time. The first scenes of the divine birth of the pharaoh are depicted in images. Here, Sahure drinks of the goddess Hathors' divine milk.

was also called "the bull of the skies," on account of the vital force of this animal, and was incarnated in the bull Mnevis.

Re' was the creator of the first divine couple, Shu and Tefnut, and also created mortals from his tears. His earthly reign extended to gods and men. And yet men revolted against Re', who had to send the goddess Hathor (called the Eye of Re') to chastise them. Generally represented as a benevolent cow, Hathor transformed herself into a furious lioness in order to sow terror and destruction among men. Because she threatened to destroy them completely, Re' was forced to intoxicate her and quell her wrath. In another version it was the lioness Sekhmet who took on the role of the angered "Eye of Re'."

The religious evolution manifested itself in architecture. All the pharaohs of the fifth dynasty except the last two erected solar temples. These open-air sanctuaries, inundated by sunlight, were modelled on the temple in Heliopolis. They were built around a platform symbolizing the primeval hillock where light first emerged from Nun, the primordial ocean. The best-preserved temple is that of King Nyuserres' (whose name means the power belongs to Re'), in Abu Gurab. It consists of a vast complex of two temples with colonnaded porticoes, linked by an oblique ramp. A squat obelisk, symbolizing the emergence of the sun, stands on a podium in a large courtyard and is surrounded by a wall with stores. In front of the obelisk, a table holds offerings. Outside the walls of the complex, a solar boat in mud brick flanks the sanctuary.

The pyramids of the pharaohs of the fifth dynasty built at Abusir are of more modest dimensions than those of their predecessors, and they are rather badly preserved. All the same, the pyramid that Unas (last king of the fifth dynasty) built in Sakkara is particularly interesting. The walls of its funerary chamber are covered with engraved hieroglyphs, painted blue. They are the oldest extant religious Egyptian texts, and reveal to us the Heliopolitan ideology at the inception of the pyramids and the solar temples. These texts contain hymns, incantations, fragments of myths and legends, and magical formulas. Together with other inscriptions found in the tombs of the sixth dynasty, they constitute what are called the *Pyramid Texts*.

These texts were meant to ensure the kings' apotheosis, and his fusion with Re'. "King Unas is on his way to heaven. Heron has taken flight in the air. ... He has embraced the sky like a falcon. ... O all-powerful sun god, your son is coming to you. ... He rules over the divine boat." In his celestial abode, the king was surrounded by his close relations, who had access, themselves, to a stellar survival.

Already under the fifth dynasty, a social evolution was underfoot. Until now reserved for members of the royal family, the highest functions were now delegated to people of more modest birth. With this change, lines of dignitaries developed. In addition, scribes formed a class of increasing importance.

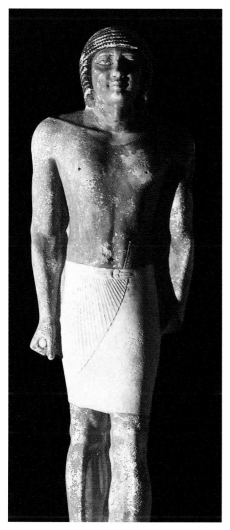

The end of the Old Kingdom

During the sixth dynasty (founded by Teti), royal power abated to the benefit of the local princes, the nomarchs, and the high functionaries. Increasingly, their duties were passed on through heredity, thereby escaping the sovereigns' control. Powerful families played an ever more important role in the kingdom. Pepi I even married two daughters of one of these families in a bid to win them over. This erosion of power eventually caused the fall of the Old Kingdom, incapable of resisting the mounting social unrest.

And yet one cannot really speak of decadence under the sixth dynasty. A brilliant civilisation continued to manifest itself in the refined art of statuary and bas-reliefs, and in literature, of which some treatises of moral precepts have survived to our day.

Under the 94-year-long reign of Pepi II (who acceded to the throne at age ten), the disintegration of the central power became more pronounced. The king organised numerous commercial expeditions – to the Sinai, to Byblos, Nubia, and the land of Punt. An explorer even brought a pygmy to the pharaohs' court. The military, however, could not adequately protect the caravans, which fell prey to Bedouin pillagers with ever increasing frequency.

The last pharaoh of the sixth dynasty was a woman, Queen Nitokris, who reigned amidst the conspiracies and succession fights that marked the end of the Old Kingdom. This queen is the subject of many legends.

One of these illustrates the troubled atmosphere of the times. Apparently, Nitokris succeeded her husband after he was killed in a conspiracy. Once enthroned, she invited the murderers to a banquet organised in a splendid underground hall with doors that opened onto the Nile. She avenged her husbands' death by drowning the guests.

Another legend claims that Nitokris finished building Mykerinos' pyramid. In this tradition, her name is amalgamated with that of the courtesan Rhodopis, "the rosy-cheeked beauty." According to Herodotus, the Greeks attributed to Rhodopis the construction of this pyramid.

The Old Kingdom ended in anarchy and social revolution. It was replaced by a period called the First Intermediate Period.

A Dignitary from the fifth dynasty

During the Old Kingdom, private statuary followed the classicism and idealism imposed by royal representations. The Egyptian canon, elaborated as early as the first dynasties, evolved very little in the course of Egyptian history until the New Kingdom. In the fifth dynasty, the statues of dignitaries, still massive, wear the short loincloth and curly wig. The eyes are often inlaid.

THE FIRST INTERMEDIATE PERIOD

The First Intermediate Period is the era of anarchy and disruption that starts with the end of the sixth dynasty around 2260 BC. It covers the period from the seventh to the tenth dynasties, including part of the eleventh dynasty, and concludes around 2040 BC. This period of social unrest, of invasions from Asia, of famine and poverty is depicted by the pessimistic writings of its time and by a later text, the *Prophecy of Neferty*. The social revolution extends to the religious domain, where we witness a kind of democratisation of the afterlife and the extension of the Osirian destiny to all the deceased.

Invasion and social revolution

The *Prophecy of Neferty* affords us precious testimony on the troubles that arose at the end of the Old Kingdom. Neferty, in effect, presents to the king a terrible picture of this agitated period.

The lector-priest Neferty starts by expressing his distress about the impending calamities and his indignation at the general indifference that meets these calamities. He sees the sun collapsing, the Nile drying up, and the riverbank becoming water. He announces foreign invasions. The Prophet sees values being turned upside down, and general disruption. To civil war is added social revolution. And, finally, Neferty predicts that a king arising from the South, "a child of Upper Egypt," will chase the Asians away and reunite the country, thus restoring law and order.

The precise events that provoked the collapse of the Old Kingdom are not well known. The Bedouins of Semitic origin from the land of Canaan, who lived off the pillaging of caravans, infiltrated the Delta. This foreign invasion and the rising social unrest undoubtedly precipitated the fall of a power already enfeebled by the growing strength of the high functionaries, reinforced by the hereditary transmission of duties. During the First Intermediate Period, the local particularities became exacerbated. The nomarchs obtained considerable power, accumulating civil and religious titles. Alliances between different nomes were made and unmade, much like among feudal lords.

Under the seventh and eighth dynasties, the pharaohs resided in Memphis but the administrative center was at Abydos. Pharaohs came and went in quick succession; no one succeeded in truly imposing himself.

The ninth and tenth dynasties established their capital in Heracleopolis Magna, in Middle Egypt. The tenth dynasty was forced to admit the reign of a parallel rival dynasty in Thebes (Upper Egypt). The frontier was constituted by This and Abydos. Already at the end of the eighth Heracleopolitan Dynasty, Antef, a prince from Thebes, had given political ambitions to his region.

Under the ninth dynasty, Thebes, in alliance with other Southern princes, formed a powerful block. Then two Theban princes, Mentuhotep and another Antef, acquired ever greater power and influence, to the point where Antef named himself pharaoh, as King Antef I. As for Mentuhotep, he was promoted pharaoh retrospectively and became the ancestor founder of the eleventh dynasty. This Theban dynasty was in perpetual struggle against the Heracleopolitan dynasty. The region of This and Abydos was conquered by each in turn. The Theban dynasty finally triumphed, under the reign of Mentuhotep II, who succeeded three kings named Antef, around 2040 BC.

The crisis of the First Intermediate Period left a deep impression in the minds of the Egyptians. The texts of the era articulated a new and quite pessimistic vision of the world. They would be read, studied, recopied, and commented upon throughout the Middle Kingdom.

Pages 36-37:

The Papyrus of Ani

The Book of the Dead, *or more precisely* Formulas for Going Out by Day, *contains around 165 chapters that collect formulas to help the deceased in the hereafter. Here, Ani asks the goddess Hathor (represented as a cow wearing the solar crown as a headdress) for her protection in the underworld, promising her his total devotion during his earthly existence.*

Funerary Art

It was customary for the Egyptians to contain the embalmed mummy inside several coffins, one each inside the other. The deceased's social status determined the number of coffins and the materials used. The outside coffin was generally of painted and varnished wood, peppered with inscriptions and formulas meant to help the deceased in his passing into the hereafter.

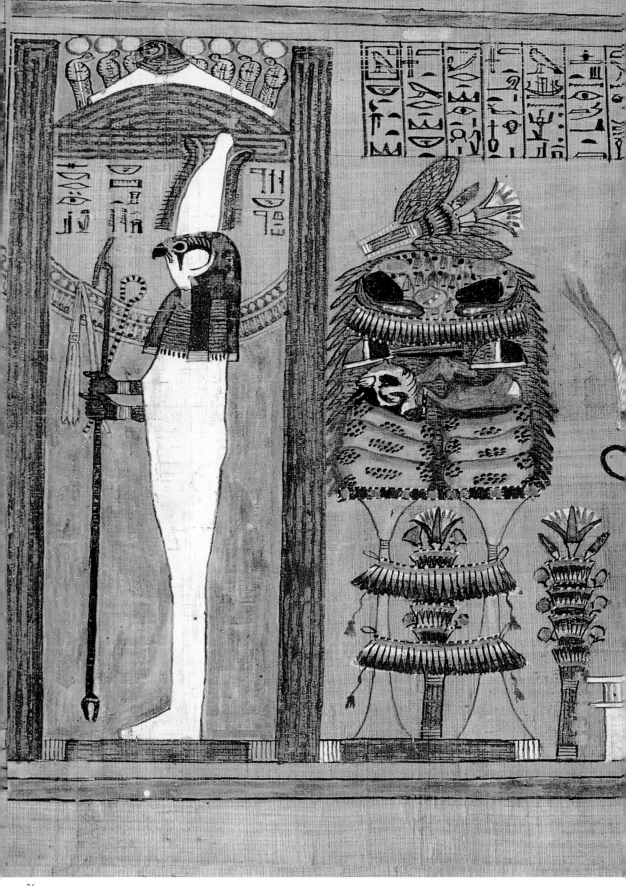

Osiris

The death and resurrection of Osiris are symbolic of his function as god of vegetation, the earth cycle, and of germination. Osiris is represented wrapped in bandages like a mummy, but his face and hands are green, like vegetables.

Thutmose III's chapel

Honoring the gods while alive to better ensure eternal survival in the hereafter remained a constant preoccupation of Egyptian thought. Thutmose III's chapel in Deir el-Bahari bears witness to his whole-hearted devotion to the Theban god Amun. Adorned with ritualistic attire, the pharaoh makes an offering of the incense and water used to purify the repast of the gods.

And yet, if these texts depict the downfall of the country and evoke the distress of the people who lived through these dramatic events, they also reveal an awakening of consciousness born of the disintegration of values.

In the *Precepts to his Son Merikare*, King Kheti III, of the 10th Heracleopolitan Dynasty, acknowledges his errors and gives his son advice for the peaceful coexistence with the Theban dynasties.

The religious evolution

The social crisis of this time was at the origin of a religious upheaval. The common man developed a consciousness of his destiny. Life in the hereafter, which had been the privilege of the pharaoh, the members of the royal family, and the high dignitaries, became accessible to all Egyptians. Simple private citizens engraved the famous *Sarcophagus Texts*

(inspired by the ancient *Pyramid Texts*) in their tombs. Later, these texts were copied into papyrus rolls that were placed inside the coffins and collected and shaped into what we call the Egyptian *Book of the Dead*.

The Osirian faith spread throughout Egypt. Osiris, the great god who died and was resuscitated, became a model for all men who hoped to prevail over death. Osiris, a very ancient god, occupied a special place among Egyptian gods. His nearly human destiny, his sufferings and his death made him accessible to men. His resurrection became a symbol of immense hope in life in the hereafter.

The oldest mentions of the cult of Osiris place him in Busiris, in the Delta, where he supplanted a local divinity, the god-king Andjety. Afterwards, in Heliopolis, he fought Re', and Heliopolitan cosmogony integrated him into the Ennead. At Memphis he was amalgamated into Sokaris, a chthonian divinity. Then, in Abydos, he replaced the god Khentamenti ("he who is in the West"), the lord

Weighing the soul

At the end of his travels the deceased must undergo the Judgment, in the presence of many gods and judges. His heart is placed on one side of a balance; on the other rests "Maat" or divine justice. He then utters what we call the "negative confession," before proclaiming his own virtues. A monster – the Devourer – is ready to swallow him in case of an unfavorable verdict. But in case of a different outcome he is guaranteed eternal happiness in the hereafter.

of the West and of the necropolis and the deceased. Osiris took over both his title and function.

The Osirian cycle of legend starts by Osiris' earthly reign as Geb's heir. As a civilising king, he taught agriculture to men and gave them law and religion. His brother Seth became jealous of him and planned to murder him. He invited Osiris to a banquet, in the company of seventy-two guests who were his accomplices. During the feast, Seth brought in a chest that he had custom-built, to Osiris' exact measurements. The guests were awed by it, and Seth promised the chest to the person who would fit perfectly when lying inside it. All the guests tried and failed to fit. At last Osiris lay inside it, filling it to perfection. At once, the guests jumped up and closed

the chest, sealed it and threw it into the Nile. Isis – Osiris' wife and sister – set out to find it, crossing all of Egypt in vain. She finally found it in the port of Byblos, where the chest confining Osiris had been transformed into a palace column. Isis returned to Egypt with her spouse's body and hid it in the Delta. There, the great magician Isis managed to conceive a son by her deceased husband. Horus was born and grew up under the shelter of papyrus groves.

The ruthless Seth, however, discovered Osiris' cadaver and cut it into 14 pieces, which he scattered all over Egypt. Isis resumed her quest and found all the pieces except one – the phallus, which had fallen into the Nile and been swallowed by an oxyrhynchus, a fish amalgamated with Seth. Assisted by her sister

Nephthys, Isis reconstituted Osiris and wrapped his body with bandages, creating the first mummy.

With the help of Thot, god of the magic Verb, she gave him life in a new form: Osiris henceforth reigned in the hereafter. His son Horus, after a mighty struggle against Seth, secured the earthly kingdom. This is why the living pharaoh is equated with Horus, son of Osiris (in turn equated with Horus, the celestial falcon), and the deceased pharaoh becomes Osiris.

Since prehistoric times Egyptians believed in survival within the tomb. Next to the body, they left provisions meant to nourish the "ka," the deceased's vital body or ethereal double. Later they would represent these provisions on the walls of the tomb. As for the "ba" (the soul-bird) that escaped from the body

at the moment of death, it was incorporated in a funerary statue of the deceased, called "ba statue," through the rite of the opening of the mouth.

During the First Intermediate Period the belief in Osirian survival developed continuously. It was thought that the deceased travelled in the Amduat or "that which is in the afterworld," where he faced numerous dangers, fought against terrible monsters and demons, and underwent all sorts of metamorphoses. *The Sarcophagus Texts* are formulations and magical incantations that the deceased had to recite to triumph over all these ordeals.

The difficult era of the First Intermediate Period concluded under the reign of the Theban Pharaoh Mentuhotep II, who overcame the Heracleopolitan dynasty and reunited Egypt.

THE MIDDLE KINGDOM

The debut of the Middle Kingdom

The majority of historians agree that the beginning of the Middle Kingdom coincides with Egypt's reunification by Mentuhotep II, around 2040 BC, roughly in the middle of the eleventh dynasty. This Theban dynasty was born during the disorder of the First Intermediate Period. It prevailed with the kings named Antef, who engaged in an active struggle against the parallel, Heracleopolitan dynasty, and against the Asians. It finally triumphed with Mentuhotep II, son of Antef III, who reigned over a country that was reunited once again.

The pharaohs of the eleventh dynasty confronted the independent, tribal Nubian dynasties, and re-established Egyptian authority over this region. They also reopened the trade route towards the Red Sea. They established their capital at Thebes. This was the birth of Thebes' greatness. Under the New Kingdom, Thebes would become one of the most prestigious cities of Antiquity.

The very name of Mentuhotep, which means "Menu is satisfied," is a reference to Thebes. Menu, in effect, was the protector god of Thebes, originally an astral divinity that was assimilated into a falcon-god and then became a warrior god, patron of Thebes. To signal the importance of his achievement, Mentuhotep II took on an epithet of Horus' with pointed significance: "he who reunited the Two Lands."

Mentuhotep II undertook a policy of cultural and economic restoration that was continued by his son, Mentuhotep III. He renovated many temples, notably at Abydos, Dendera, and Tod. At Gebelein, near Thebes, he built a temple – today in ruins – decorated with scenes commemorating the battles fought in reuniting the country and the victories against the Nubians and the Asians. He organised many expeditions to the mines and quarries, to Aswan and Nubia, to the exotic markets of Punt and the Phoenician coast.

On the rocky amphitheatre at Deir el-Bahari, on the western shore of Thebes, Mentuhotep III built himself a grand funerary complex, now in ruins. It prefigures the splendid "Temple of a Million Years" of Queen Hatshepsut, for which it probably served as a model. And yet its conception remains loyal to the spirit of the Old Kingdom, where the funerary architecture combined temple and pyramid.

From the temple in the valley, a route climbing westwards led to a vast court planted with trees. From there, a rising ramp built along the axis of the route led to the first terrace, supported by a colonnade of square columns of sandstone that rose on the court on either side of the ramp. A second superposed terrace surrounded on three sides by a colonnade supported the pyramid.

A gallery descended from the great court to Mentuhotep's cenotaph, where some furniture and a seated statue of the king were found. From a peristyle court situated behind the pyramid, at the height of the first terrace, a corridor led to the cliff where the funerary cave was hewn. Housed inside was an empty sarcophagus. The complex included also a hypostyle hall sunk into the cliff, flanked by a small chapel, and the tombs of princesses and high dignitaries. The king cut a collective tomb into the nearby rocky terrain for sixty of his soldiers killed in battle.

The eleventh dynasty ended with Mentuhotep IV, whose reign was disturbed by a civil war. The vizier Amenemes or Amenemhet put an end to the civil war and took power.

The god Min

This detail of a column from the White Chapel of Senusret I at Karnak shows the exceptional quality of the relief, where all the details are finely chiselled. This is the ithyphallic god of fertility Min, wearing tight-fitting linens and always depicted with the right arm bent behind the head and holding a whip.

The apogee: the 12th dynasty

Around 1991 BC, Amenemhet I, Mentuhotep IV's former vizier, founded the 12th dynasty (1991 – 1785 BC). This dynasty, marked by kings named Amenemhet and Senusret, was one of the most glorious of Egyptian history.

The sovereigns of the 12th dynasty settled their capital in Lisht, south of Memphis, a strategic point located at the junction of Upper and Lower Egypt. Incidentally, the Egyptian name of Lisht was Itjtawy: "he who seizes the Two Lands."

The 12th dynasty marks the start of a new era, a period of political, cultural, and religious renaissance. The kings undertook a policy of conquest, not out of imperialism but of concern for the defence of the territory. They surrounded themselves with a line of vassal states meant to protect Egypt from all foreign invasions; the memories of the First Intermediate Period endured.

They integrated Lower Nubia into the kingdom by using a system of fortresses. They controlled the Libyan oases.

Closer ties were developed with Byblos, ruled by dynasties of very Egyptianised princes.

Trade with Syro-Palestine and even the Aegean world flourished a great deal. The sovereigns of the 12th dynasty organised the exploitation of the Fayum, formerly covered with marshes. They encouraged the growth of literature; texts that would become "classics" of Egyptian literature date from this era.

There was also a renewal of religious fervor around the gods Osiris, Ptah, and Amun.

Amenemhet I, whose name means "Amen is at the Head," is the inheritor both of the great challenges to power that marked the First Intermediate Period and the troubles that accompanied his ascent to the throne.

Amenemhet I facilitated the recruitment of administrators, while at the same time continuing the Old Kingdom practice of rule by great monarchic families. He consolidated the frontiers with military operations in Nubia, Palestine, and Libya.

He built the "Prince's Walls," a series of fortifications meant to protect the access to the Delta by the Asians with permanent garrisons.

To avoid the troubles of succession, he named his son Senusret I co-regent during a period of ten years. Despite all that, he was murdered after a harem intrigue.

Senusret I kissing Ptah

In this relief from Karnak, King Senusret I bears the royal headdress (the nemes) with the uraeus on his brow. He kisses the god Ptah, clad in his mummy-shaped sheath. This example of a mystical alliance between a god and a pharaoh illustrates a much-pursued theme of divine Egyptian iconography.

He was buried at his pyramid in Lisht, surrounded by tombs of close relatives (located inside the delimiting walls of the complex) and of about a hundred mastabas of dignitaries (located outside the complex walls).

Senusret I then found himself pharaoh in an atmosphere of political crisis. It was while returning from an expedition against the Libyans that he learned of his father's murder.

He hastened home immediately and avoided civil war. He set out to reinforce his legitimacy. He surrounded himself with scholars and instigated works of "propaganda" such as the *Story of Sinuhe*, which elegantly recounts the theme of royal clemency, and *The Instructions of Amenemhet I to his son*, a kind of apocryphal political testament.

Senusret I undertook an expansionist policy. In Nubia, he went well beyond the second cataract. He started the construction of fortifications, notably at Buhen and Mirgissa, to protect the country from the Sudanese of the Kingdom of Kush, a territory located between the second and fourth cataracts. At Mirgissa, an official magician bewitched statuettes depicting Egypt's enemies. From one fortress to another, permanent troops communicated using smoke signals.

This system was reinforced with administrative steps: Sarenput, the prince of Aswan, was named governor of Nubia, and the prince of Assiut was charged with the administration of Kerma.

Senusret I's internal policies remained traditional. The king maintained the feudal system of the nomarchs. Though hereditary transmission endured, each individual passing on of power had to be approved by the sovereign. To ensure the stability of the realm, Senusret I named his son Amenemhet II co-regent.

The king undertook a vast programme of temple restoration throughout Egypt. He also built new temples, notably a temple dedicated to Hathor and another to Atum at Heliopolis, and erected statues and obelisks.

The White Chapel

Composed of reconstituted blocks found in the third pylon in Karnak, this little pavilion built by Senusret I during the Middle Kingdom remains a jewel of divine pharaonic architecture. Named White Chapel on account of the purity of the limestone that was used, the edifice seems to have had the function of chapel-cum-shrine for the god Amun-Min.

Nofret

The granite statue of Nofret, Senusret II's wife, illustrate the new trends in jewellery of the Middle Kingdom. She wears a long, sheath-like strap dress that exposes the breasts, and a stiff, curly wig topped with the royal uraeus. In the Middle Kingdom the ears, always uncovered, are depicted bigger than normal.

He built the White Chapel at Karnak, which is also referred to as "the barque shrine". It is the only monument of the Middle Kingdom for which all building blocks have been recovered, allowing for a complete reconstruction of the edifice. A colossal statue of the king in white limestone was discovered at Karnak.

Senusret I was buried at Lisht. His funerary complex lies south of Amenemhet I's, and it contains a funerary temple, small pyramids where relatives were buried, the royal pyramid (60 meters tall: 197 ft.), and mastabas located outside the walls of the complex. Statues of Osiris and of the king, as well as jewellery, vases, and toiletries, were found on the site.

Amenemhet II, the son of Senusret I, increased commercial relations with Punt, the Syro-Palestinian coast, and even Crete and Cyprus, undoubtedly through the Phoenicians. In Upper Egypt, in the foundation soil at the temple of Tod, numerous gold and silver objects, some of Aegean origin, were found.

For three years, Amenhemhet II made his son, Senusret II, co-regent. He was buried at Dahshur, south of Sakkara, in a pyramid of white Turah limestone. Its framework was filled with bricks and sand, and today the pyramid is very much in ruins.

Administrative reform took place under Senusret II's reign. The king created a new hierarchy with new duties. Little by little the nomarchic lineages disappeared. The nome administrators were replaced by city governors, supervised by men who answered to the vizier. The kingdom was divided into three regions.

Senusret II undertook the exploitation of the Fayum (from "pa-yum," the ocean), located southwest of Memphis. This great oasis used to be covered with swamps where only intrepid hunters ventured.

To regularise the flow of water, a lock was built at Illahun; the great lake Moeris (today lake Qarun) was levelled; a dam was erected; finally, canals were dug. A large, well-irrigated fertile plain with regulated hunting and fishing zones and a bird sanctuary was the result.

Senusret II built his funerary complex at Illahun. The pyramid was 50 meters (164 ft.) high. The king's red granite sarcophagus was discovered in the funerary chamber. North of the pyramid were eight rock-cut tombs and the queen's little pyramid, where magnificent princesses' jewels were found. They attested to the refined art and talent of the goldsmiths of the time.

King Mentuhotep

This mostly intact sandstone statue, found in Mentuhotep's funerary chapel in Deir el-Bahari, surprises the viewer with its massiveness. Mentuhotep is seated in an Osirian attitude on a throne devoid of any ornamentation. He's wearing the white Heb-Sed dress, the red crown of Lower Egypt, and the false beard of Osiris. It is one of the few existing examples of polychrome royal statues.

Senusret III

Under the reign of Senusret III, art abandons the idealised canon established during the Old Kingdom in favor of a much more naturalistic depiction of the royal person. The pharaoh, shown aged, his features drawn, with prominent rings under the eyes, reveals the fatigue accumulated over years of exercising his power and a trace of bitterness in his long face.

Senusret III, son of Senusret II, completed the integration of Lower Nubia into the kingdom. He needed four military expeditions to get the better of the local populations. He finished the system of fortresses; erected a stele that marked the frontier at Semna and on which was engraved a text glorifying the king; and established strict control over the movements of the Nubians.

The commercial expeditions themselves were also controlled. To ease the passage of the boats between the rocks of the first cataract, he had a canal dug at Sehel. Under the New Kingdom, Senusret III was divinised in Nubia.

Senusret III was buried in a pyramid that was called the "Black Pyramid" because its bricks were made of Nile silt. His funerary complex is at Dahshur, but he had a cenotaph built at Abydos.

His successor Amenemhet III maintained regular commercial relations with Nubia.

These relations were perfectly controlled, thanks to the system developed by Senusret III. He strengthened the Egyptian ties with the Phoenician city-states, particularly with Byblos but also with Tyre, Sidon, and Ugarit. The Byblos sovereigns were very Egyptianised. In the tomb of Abi-Shemou, a nomarch contemporaneous with Amenemhet III, the following objects were found: a gold diadem decorated with the uraeus and the ankh (the Egyptian cross symbolising life); a gold pectoral inscribed with Amenemhet III's cartouche; ointment vases; and Egyptian boxes made of gold or obsidian.

The tiara of the Byblos kings resembled the crown of Upper Egypt. The Phoenician princes spoke Egyptian. The maritime commerce between the Phoenician and Egypt cities flourished. Egypt imported large quantities of cedar wood from Mount Lebanon for the construction of its sailboats.

Amenemhet III built a "black" pyramid, like Senusret III's, where a royal sarcophagus made of pink granite was discovered. And yet it was at his pyramid in Aware, in the Fayum, that he was buried. His funerary temple, rising south of the pyramid, was the famous Labyrinth, thus named by the Greeks on account of the countless halls and colonnades that constituted it.

At least that is what Greek tradition holds; the building is too ruined to give us an idea of its original appearance. Together with the pyramids, the temple to Amun in Thebes, and the Colossi of Memnon, the Labyrinth was one of the most celebrated Egyptian monuments in Herodotus' time. He visited it and was dazzled.

According to Strabon, a visitor who explored it alone would not be able to find his way in or out.

At Tanis, two statues of Amenemhet III were discovered, one as a sphinx.

At Medinet Madi, in the Fayum, Amenemhet III started building a small temple dedicated to the crocodile Sobk, god of the Fayum; to Norus; and to Renenutet, the local serpent goddess and protector of the harvests. It was his successor, Amenemhet IV (who was possibly his nephew), who finished its construction.

The last sovereign of the 12th dynasty was a woman, Queen Sobekneferu (or Skemiophris), daughter of Amenemhet III. She ascended to the throne following the death of her husband, Amenemhet IV.

The Middle Kingdom, and particularly the 12th dynasty, was a very fecund period for Egyptian literature. Some great works of the time became "classics," recopied and studied in Egypt up to the end of the New Kingdom. The texts are of contrasting types: moral precepts, hymns, and above all adventure tales and yarns.

The *Instructions of Amenemhet I to his son* is both a political legitimisation of Senusret I and a bitter moral report that is still very close to the disillusions of the First Intermediate Period.

The famous *Prophecy of Neferty*, which we mentioned before, is a work of the Middle Kingdom. It seems plausible that its first draft goes back to Amenemhet I, the founder of the dynasty.

Neferty announces the arrival of a saviour king, a native of Upper Egypt, named Ameny (a shortened version of Amenemhet), and the construction of the "Prince's Walls," the series of fortifications erected by Amenemhet I.

The *Tale of the Oasis Dweller,* also known as *The Peasant's Complaint* or *Tale of the Eloquent Peasant* is of a very different genre. This rather long work highlights the taste of the Egyptians of the Middle Kingdom for rambling discourse. In the eras that followed, this work was less appreciated.

Written in the beginning of the 12th dynasty, the *Tale of the Shipwrecked Sailor* belongs to a very particular genre, widespread in Antiquity. It is a fabulous story like those that sailors through the times love to tell upon returning from distant and dangerous travels, freely embellishing their adventures.

The *Tale of Sinuhe* is the masterpiece of Egyptian literature. This adventure yarn was greatly appreciated in Egypt from the 12th to the 20th Dynasties: today, its charming narrative and the lively style still seduce contemporary readers.

The development of the Fayum under the 12th dynasty increased the popularity of the protecting divinity of this place, the crocodile-god Sobk (Soukhos in Greek). His cult spread throughout Egypt from the Middle Kingdom onwards.

The crocodile is at once an aquatic, chthonian, and solar symbol. Sobk is tied to Re', as the crocodile rose from the primordial waters of the Fayum much as the sun rose from the Nun.

The Egyptians compared Lake Moeris to a liquid sky. It was said that the sun, having aged, took the form of a crocodile in order to hide in the lake.

In his temple at Shedet (Crocodilopolis for the Greeks), Sobk was thus greeted every morning by the priests: "Greetings to you, Sobk the Crocodilopolitan, Re', Horus, powerful god… greetings to you, risen from the primordial waters." In each city where Sobk was venerated, a sacred crocodile was tamed and kept.

The three great gods of the Middle Kingdom were Ptah, Osiris, and Amun-Re. Ptah, the creator god of Memphis, remained very important. He was depicted in human form, cast in a tight sheath like a mummy, from which only his hands holding a scepter emerged.

Senusret I

The beginning of the Middle Kingdom is marked by an abundant artistic production, always of very good quality. Here, Senusret I, wearing the white crown of Upper Egypt, is depicted in a standing pose, appearing to walk. The statue is made of wood, which is quite exceptional considering how badly this material has survived over the centuries.

The bearers of offerings at Tanis

Formerly considered a Hyksos work of art, this statue group in fact depicts King Amenemhet III offering Nile goods to the gods. The strange style of this work in granite, with people wearing stiff wigs and long beards, bears no resemblance to Egyptian art.

Ptah was connected to Osiris through an ancient god of the Memphite necropolis, Sokaris, whom they both had assimilated. Ptah was the patron of craftsmen.

The cult of Osiris had greatly expanded during the First Intermediate Period. Osiris was the master of Abydos since the sixth dynasty. The Antef kings of the eleventh dynasty had turned this sanctuary into the most important center of the Osirian cult. Under the Middle Kingdom, Abydos became the first holy city of Egypt. This probably represented the desire of the kings of the era to be related to the pharaohs of Egypt and to consecrate the triumph of the new Osirian beliefs. Moreover, from the time of Senusret III onwards, many cenotaphs were built at Abydos.

The Osirian legend authenticates the primacy of this sanctuary. In fact, according to one of its versions, as Isis found each part of Osiris' dismembered body she would bury the part where she found it, and each of these "tombs" of the god became an Osirian sanctuary. It is at Abydos that Osiris' head was supposedly found.

Abydos was the theatre of the great annual festival of Osiris, in which the god's mysteries were celebrated.

The Middle Kingdom witnessed the birth of the official cult of Amun, who until then was an obscure local god, venerated at Karnak. The Theban pharaohs decided to impose this local divinity. Thanks to a syncretism with Re, they quickly managed to render Amun a prestigious god. Amun soon became the sovereign god of the Egyptian pantheon, all the while accommodating the powerful Heliopolis clergy. To establish Amun's theology, they borrowed from the three great cosmogonic systems, and even from the personality of the ithyphallic god Min, master of foreign lands and of regeneration. A neighboring vulture-goddess, Mut, was associated to Amun, and she became his wife. A lunar god, Khons, became his son.

It is certain that Amun, "the hidden one," was originally a celestial god, master of wind and air. Though he had his sacred animals, the ram and the goose, he was usually depicted in human form, wearing a crown of two high feathers, symbol of the gods of the sky. He was promoted to secret god of the beginnings (unknown even to the other gods), vital breath, creative cosmic force, intangible and invisible:

"O you who were the first to be, at the first time,
Amun who came into existence at the beginning,
We do not know where you come from…
…O god who himself shaped the egg from which he would emerge…"

"He is too secret for one to reveal his glory,
Too big for one to profit from questioning him,
Too powerful for one to hope to know him."

S. Sauneron)

The worship of Amun brought about the development of a large clergy devoted to his service. Amenemhet I instituted four servants of Amun, of which one was the high priest; four "divine fathers"; and a dozen "pure priests" who performed the daily rites around the statue of the god. The Amun clergy would play a dominant role in the New Kingdom.

The most glorious period of the Middle Kingdom ended with the 12th dynasty and Queen Sobekneferu. After her came the disorder of the 13th and 14th dynasties that triggered the Second Intermediate Period.

THE SECOND INTERMEDIATE PERIOD

With Queen Sobekneferu, the last pharaoh of the 12th dynasty, a great Egyptian era came to a close. Then another sombre period opened, one of the least well-known of Egyptian history. The country again underwent foreign invasion, division, and the reign of parallel dynasties.

Opinions diverge on the beginning of the Second Intermediate Period. Some have it start with the advent of the 13th dynasty in 1784 BC, but there was no real rupture between the 12th dynasty and the beginning of the 13th. Others choose the capture of Memphis by the Hyksos in 1650 BC to mark the launch of the Second Intermediate Period, but this date seems equally arbitrary. In fact, both the infiltration of Egypt by the Hyksos and a crisis of succession already affecting the 13th dynasty were determining factors.

The loss of power

The passage from the 12th to the 13th dynasty took place without disarray, and without notable economic and administrative change. The institutions continued to function as in the previous dynasty, the commercial exchanges were maintained, and the work of building monuments went on unabated.

Nevertheless, the situation was deteriorating. The 12th dynasty was characterised by great dynastic stability; the succession of the pharaohs was familial and proceeded without problems. But the 13th dynasty saw some 60 kings between about 1784 and 1650 BC. Some reigned for a few years, others for a few months. Among these sovereigns, many were men of modest birth, military men, or foreigners of Asian origin. This crisis of succession, for reasons we are ignorant of,

did not affect the stability of the high functions. There were lineages of viziers, like that of Ankhu, son of a vizier and father of two viziers, Iymeru and Resseneb. Because of the rapid succession of pharaohs, Ankhu carried out his functions under several reigns, including those of Sebekhotep II and Sebekhotep III.

Little by little, the territory controlled by the sovereigns of the 13th dynasty diminished. They lost Nubia. Apparently following a revolt in the marshes of the Delta, two independent kingdoms, ruled by two parallel monarchies, were formed. Together they constitute the 14th dynasty, contemporaneous with the 13th.

The first of these independent kingdoms was created at Xois, in the north-western region of the Delta, perhaps already under Sebekhotep IV (a pharaoh of the 13th dynasty who ruled from 1730 to 1723 BC).

The second kingdom, located on the north-eastern region of the Delta, was founded around 1720 BC by Nehesy, "the Nubian," at Avaris, a river port with a high concentration of Asians dedicated to commerce with Byblos.

This 14th dynasty reigning over the eastern Delta was supplanted by the Hyksos. From Avaris, the Hyksos – who probably began establishing themselves in Egypt around 1730 BC – spread their domination of Egypt. These events probably took place under the reign of Dedumes, a pharaoh of the 13th dynasty.

Egypt under the Hyksos yoke

What is the origin then of these "barbarians" who invaded Egypt, where they settled for about a century? The name "Hyksos" is a Greek term that comes from the Egyptian expression "hekau khasut," meaning "princes from foreign lands."

They were Asians, most likely Semitic peoples chased out of Anatolia, Mesopotamia, Mitanni, and Iran, who first went to Canaan, and then to the Nile Delta.

Participants in the great Indo-European migration of the 20th to the 18th centuries BC, they swept out of the north when the Persians, the people of the Medes, the Hittites, and the Kassites expelled their native Semitic populations.

The first Hyksos penetration of the eastern Delta took place around 1730-1720 BC, under the 13th and 14th Egyptian dynasties. They settled in Avaris, which they turned into a fortified city.

Their chief, Salitis, reigned as the first pharaoh of the 15th dynasty, after being crowned at Memphis in 1650 BC.

The 15th dynasty was therefore a Hyksos dynasty that totally dominated the eastern Delta. In the rest of Lower Egypt, the Hyksos entrusted vassal Asian administrators with power, and in Middle Egypt they installed small kingdoms run by Egyptians that collaborated with the enemy.

These allied monarchs, Asians and Egyptians, formed the 16th dynasty, which controlled Lower Egypt and part of Middle Egypt.

Parallel to the 15th and 16th dynasties, a Theban dynasty – the 17th dynasty, directly succeeding the 13th Egyptian dynasty after the Hyksos conquest in 1650 BC – reigned over Upper Egypt and part of Middle Egypt. Its kings paid tribute to the Hyksos.

Some of them tried to fight the invader, but because their military means were very inferior to the Hyksos', they were unsuccessful. The real war of liberation would not start until Kames (or Kamose).

The Egyptians retained terrible recollections of this period of occupation, perhaps blackening the picture a bit and exaggerating the barbaric nature of the Hyksos: "…from the regions of the east, invaders of obscure race marched in confidence of victory against our land.

By main force they easily overpowered the rulers of the land, they then burned our cities ruthlessly, razed to the ground the temples of the gods, and treated all the natives with a cruel hostility, massacring some and leading into slavery the wives and children of others." (Manetho, quoted by the historian Josephus.)

The Tanis Sphinx

Four maned sphinxes in black granite were found in the Tanis excavations. Despite the multiple usurpations of the Hyksos kings and of Ramesses II, the style attests to its origin during the reign of Amenemhet III in the Middle Kingdom. Here, the head of the Sphinx is surrounded by an authentic lion mane, rather than the traditional royal headdress.

Nevertheless, this era was not entirely negative. The Hyksos introduced new weapons into Egypt: iron axes and daggers, and, most importantly, the horse-drawn chariot. Far from despising Egyptian civilisation, they adopted some of its mores. They borrowed the titles and ceremonials of the pharaohs, and took Egyptian names which they wrote in hieroglyphs and surrounded with a cartouche. They adopted Avaris's god, Seth, master of tempest and of the desert, which they assimilated to their gods Sutekh and Baal. In addition, the Asian divinities Baal and Astarte were introduced into the Egyptian pantheon. The Hyksos worshipped Re', who took on a more warrior-like aspect, analogous to the Asian solar gods. The Egyptians, in turn, gave renewed importance to the cult of Thot. He was the lunar god, master of speech and writing, and was worshipped in the manner of the moon god of the Semitic nomads.

The penultimate Hyksos king, Apophis (or Apopi), shows up in a story: *The Dispute of Apopi and Sekenenre*. It is believed that Sekenenre Tao waged war against the Hyksos. In any case, his mummy bears the traces of several fatal injuries to the head.

Sekenenre Tao married his sister Ahhotep ("may the moon be satisfied"). Two of their sons, Kamose and Ahmose, led the war of liberation; it was Ahmose who triumphed over the Hyksos and reunited Egypt.

Kamose – Sekenenre's successor – decided to fight the Asians against the objections of his Council, which wished to preserve the peace. He seized the town of Nefrusy and took the combat to the outskirts of Avaris. But he was forced to return south and wage war against the king of Kush, who had allied himself with Apopi. Kamose's brother, Ahmose, succeeded him. He liberated Egypt, thus inaugurating a new era; he is considered the founder of the 18th dynasty.

THE NEW KINGDOM: THE CONQUEST

Around 1570 BC Ahmose, the liberator and founder of the prestigious 18th dynasty, inaugurated a new era of greatness for unified Egypt. The first sovereigns of the 18th dynasty were conquerors and builders, and they transformed Thebes into a capital of an immense empire.

A new ideology animated the pharaohs of the incipient empire: henceforth the king was seen as a victor who assimilated the magical powers of the cosmos. He was seen as the son and "beloved" of Amun-Re', the warrior god who remained by the king's side in battle and protected him.

The ascent of the 18th dynasty was an era of expansion, glory, and wealth for Egypt, undoubtedly the most brilliant of its history. The numerous conquests earned Egypt immense loot carried home by the victorious army, as well as rich tribute paid by the subjugated peoples.

This affluence allowed the construction of multiple grand monuments to the greater glory of Amun and the splendor of his city, Thebes "of the one hundred gates," thus named by the Greeks on account of the monumental gates of its temples, the pylons.

Ahmose the Liberator

When Prince Ahmose ("born of the moon") succeeded his brother Kamose, Egypt was still under the Hyksos yoke, despite the war of liberation led by the fervid Kamose. It was Ahmose who would bear the title of "Liberator of Egypt."

His labors, which changed the face of Egyptian history, established this pharaoh as the founder of the 18th dynasty and of the New Kingdom, even though there was familial continuity with the 17th dynasty.

It appears that Ahmose was still a child when he ascended to the throne around 1750 BC. His mother Ahhotep ("may the moon be satisfied") ensured that the regency was run competently. She held the role of regent while the king was absent on military campaigns. Her political acumen was admired by her son Ahmose. Other women would play eminent political roles in the court of the pharaohs of the 18th dynasty.

We have some information about the war of liberation and Ahmose's campaigns, thanks to the text of the *Autobiography of Ahmose, son of Abana*, which the latter had engraved on the walls of his tomb.

This soldier native of El Kab, son of a soldier of Sekenenre Tao, fought under Ahmose, Amenhotep I, and Thutmose I. He demonstrated great courage, was rewarded many times with the gold of valor (the king's reward of gold necklaces given to his bravest soldiers), engaged in combat up to a very advanced age, and finished his career wealthy and honored. Ahmose, son of Abana, had just started a family when he had to follow the king in his march on Avaris.

First the sovereign took Heliopolis and Sile, then he lay siege to Avaris, the Hyksos capital. Ahmose, son of Abana, distinguished himself during the taking of Avaris, both on land and on water during combat over the canals of Avaris. To prove his bravery, he carried off the amputated hands of enemies killed in battle.

The pharaoh, upon hearing of this, offered him the gold of valor, for having himself in battle. He brought back captives, and the king gave him these captives as servants. After the fall of Avaris, the Hyksos were expelled from Egypt.

King Ahmose, a prudent warrior, chased the disoriented enemy all the way to Canaan, where the siege of Sharouen lasted three years, and to the Phoenician ports beyond.

Thutmose III

Among the many statues of the great pharaoh Thutmose III, this one undoubtedly remains the most remarkable. This profile, with the slightly hooked nose and sharp smile, is among the greatest masterpieces of all Egyptian statuary. This courtly and expressive art blossomed during the 18th dynasty.

Ahmose was acclaimed as the liberator of Egypt. But he was forced to return to war in Nubia, which had been recaptured by Kamose, in order to put down rebellions. He subjugated the South and placed Nubia under the authority of a governor, Thure.

Ahmose undertook administrative reforms, replacing the nomarchs with reliable men. He put the economy back on its feet, reopened the mines and quarries, and built monuments in Upper Egypt.

The Valley of the Kings

Amenhotep I, in concert with his mother Ahmose-Nefertari, conceived a grand project of gathering the tombs of the pharaohs in a new location. He built a road piercing the chosen setting, a desert wadi in the heart of a rocky amphitheatre on the western shore of Thebes. Thus was born what would become the prestigious Valley of the Kings. Its funereal atmosphere still overwhelms and fascinates the modern traveller.

His wife, Ahmose-Nefertari, was a great queen, closely linked with Ahmose's achievements. More than a councillor, she was "the one who presides over the whole of the Two Lands," taking the role of an actual co-regent. She even temporarily held the title of Amun's Second Servant (that is, Amun's Second Prophet).

This title was habitually reserved for men, but she enjoyed all of the prerogatives and rich entitlements associated with it. She was the first queen to receive the designation of Divine Wife.

Ahmose's reign was marked by the renewed importance of Amun, rendered a universal god by the sovereigns of the 18th dynasty, and by his sanctuary at Karnak, which dazzled the ancient world. There remains little of the monuments erected by Ahmose. The king developed Amun's clergy and gave much importance to the High Priest (or Amun's first servant) who, besides his religious functions, was also permitted to hold a high temporal office.

One of the stelae that Ahmose erected celebrates him as "son of Amun-Re'," the sovereign who reunited the North and the South, and whose power extends over foreign lands, far outside the Egyptian frontiers.

At Abydos, he built a cenotaph for himself and for his grandmother Tetisheri. His actual tomb remains unknown, but his mummy was found in the hiding place at Deir el-Bahari, south of the temple of Hatshepsut. Many royal mummies of the New Kingdom were gathered here for protection against tomb pillagers.

Amenhotep I

Amenhotep I, son of Ahmose and Queen Ahmose-Nefertari, rose to the throne around 1557 BC. He continued his father's military work and his policy of restoration. The *Autobiography of Ahmose, son of Abana* mentions an important expedition to suppress rebellions in Nubia. Amenhotep I created the office of viceroy of the South, or "royal son, governor of the lands of the South." He invested Thure, already governor of the South under Ahmose, with the office. He also instituted a governorship in the west to oversee the Libyan oases.

The pharaoh inaugurated the Valley of the Kings by having Ineni build his funerary temple, flanked by his mother Ahmose-Nefertari's temple, at Dra Abu el-Naga. His temple was cut into the rock of a nearby mountain. This hypogeum was constructed in the form that all the tombs of the 18th dynasty kings would end up taking. The tombs are composed of a descending corridor inside the cliff, with a chamber at the half-point, a well, and two galleries, the second of which leads to the burial vault. Amenhotep's mummy, however, was found in the hiding place at Deir el-Bahari.

Amenhotep I was divinised, as was Ahmose-Nefertari, as patron of the necropolis. The workers and artisans of the new village of Deir el-Medineh, whose guild he probably established, worshipped him in a particular manner. He was even believed to give oracles through a priest. The village of Deir el-Medineh was inhabited by all who participated in the construction of royal tombs: workers, painters, scribes, and their families. The excavations have revealed the houses of these workers, their chapels, their tombs, legal documents, accounts, letters, literary texts used by schoolchildren and their masters, inventories of materials, tools, and texts mentioning strikes: all of those things which constituted the life of the site and village.

In the temple at Karnak, Amenhotep I and his architect Ineni built a shrine in alabaster for the sacred barque. The shrine was found in pieces in the foundations of the third pylon (erected by Amenhotep III) and entirely reconstructed. The king also built a large gate in white limestone south of Amun's temple, part of which was discovered in the foundations of Thutmose III's temple.

Thutmose I the Conqueror

At his death, around 1530 BC, Amenhotep I left no son born of the Great Royal Wife. His successor, Thutmose I, "born of Thut," seems to be the son of a concubine, Senseneb. Not much is known about the new pharaoh's wife, a princess named Ahmes. Some speculate that she was the daughter of Amenhotep and the Great Royal Wife, which would make her a half-sister of Thutmose, who married her to legitimise his ascent to the throne. Others believe Ahmes was a daughter of Ahmose and Ahmose-Nefertari, which would make her one of Amenhotep I's sisters.

Thutmose I was a great conqueror. He led several campaigns in the North as well as in the South. Beginning in the second year of his reign, he campaigned in the South and crushed a Nubian revolt. He sang his victory in a hymn sculpted on the rocks of the Sudan.

According to the *Autobiography of Ahmose, son of Abana*, there seems to have been two revolts in the South. The sovereign divided Nubia into five principalities, entrusting their governorship to subjugated Nubians. Then he waged war in the land of Kush, advancing beyond the fourth cataract. Upon his return he had the canal at Sehel cleared.

In the North, Ahmose, son of Abana, tells us, Thutmose did battle in Retenu (Syria) and in the land of Canaan.

Pages 60-61:
The Dromos at Karnak

To connect two buildings, the Egyptians often built a dromos, a lane bordered by sphinxes in the prolonged main axis of the temple. The lane leading from the second pylon at Karnak to the temple of Mut, a goddess associated with the god Amun, was bordered by a series of very beautiful sphinxes with rams' heads.

Hathor's Chapel

At Deir el-Bahari, two transversal halls precede Hathor's sanctuary, cut into the rocky cliff. Some of the pillars or columns in these halls are topped with capitals bearing the effigy of the goddess Hathor, with her feminine face surrounded with two cow's ears and capped with a heavy wig. A little kiosk sheltering two solar cobras rests on her head.

Ahmose-Nefertari played a great role in the religious domain. With her son Amenhotep I, she took part in creating the "Ritual of the Daily Divine Cult." The queen was divinised as patron of the Theban necropolis. In her representations, her skin is often black like Anubis', guardian of the necropolis, and sometimes Osiris', lord of the West and of the dead.

He marched up to the Euphrates, and waged combat in the land of Naharina, on the western bank of the Euphrates, most likely against the people of Mittani, who would become Egypt's main adversaries in Asia.

Besides being a conquering pharaoh, Thutmose I was also a builder. He devoted himself to enlarging and beautifying the temple at Karnak with the help of his designer Ineni. This architect, already very active under Amenhotep I, was also the king's great financier and administrator of Amun's temple.

Thutmose and Ineni surrounded Karnak's primitive temple with a new wall and peristyle. Colossal statues of the king, depicted as Osiris and holding the scepter and flail, were placed in this peristyle. Then they erected two new pylons, today called the fourth and fifth pylons, which were covered in white Tura limestone. They built a hypostyle hall with cedar wood columns. Two obelisks in pink granite, with a golden point, rose in front of the fourth pylon.

For his burial place, Thutmose I adopted the site chosen by Amenhotep I. His funerary complex was conceived by Ineni, and its plan differed from that of the classical funerary complex. This new plan would be followed by the other pharaohs of the 18th dynasty. The temple was totally separated from the tomb and built at the edge of the desert. It was similar to a temple to a god, with pylons, a hypostyle hall, and a sanctuary, the Greek "naos."

The tomb was cut into the rock of a cliff, like a hypogeum, in the Valley of the Kings. A corridor descended towards a hall decorated with friezes and the chamber that housed the royal sarcophagus. The walls were decorated with passages from the *Book of Amduat*, a contemporary composition of excerpts from the *Pyramid Texts* and the *Sarcophagus Texts*. This book, together with the Book of Gates and the *Book of Caverns,* was much prized during the New Kingdom. The decoration of the tombs made generous use of it, showing the journey of the deceased as he encounters monstrous characters, and finally culminates in his union with Re's destiny (crossing the heavens) and with Osiris' destiny (travelling in the underworld).

Thutmose I's mummy was discovered in the hiding place at Deir el-Bahari.

With Thutmose I's death, a new dynastic problem arose. The king did not leave a son of the right lineage—born of the Great Royal Wife. The two sons that Queen Ahmes gave him were dead. It was the son of a concubine or a secondary wife called Mutnofret, a woman of royal blood, who acceded to the throne under the name of Thutmose II. To legitimise his throne, he married his half-sister Hatshepsut, daughter of Thutmose I and the Great Royal Wife Ahmes.

During his short reign, Thutmose II managed to maintain the empire. He repressed a Sudanese revolt, but did not personally direct the military expedition, as was the custom among the pharaohs. His constitution was weak and his health delicate. There was also a campaign in Palestine about which we know almost nothing.

Thutmose II's mummy attests to an early death, probably between the ages of twenty-five and thirty.

The Temple of the Thutmoses

Besides the Royal Pavilion and the funerary temple of Ramesses III, the complex at Medinet Habu includes an earlier temple, from the 18th dynasty, that was started by Amenhotep I and was continually enlarged through Thutmose III's reign. In this Ramesside setting, where the colossal prevails, the temple of the Thutmoses, elegant but of small dimensions, seems somewhat overpowered in this mass of gigantic buildings.

The pyramidion of Hatshepsut's obelisk

Of Queen Hatshepsut's two obelisks at Karnak, only the northern one still stands. The second one now lies near the sacred lake, allowing one to admire its summit (or pyramidion). The god Amun of Thebes, wearing his high headdress with two feathers and the false beard of the gods, protects the queen, who kneels in front of him. The quality of the relief attests to the mastery of the artists of the 18th dynasty.

Queen Hatshepsut

When Thutmose II died, around 1504 BC, he also did not leave a son born of his union with Hatshepsut, the Great Royal Wife, although he did have two daughters: Neferure, whose preceptor was Ahmose Pen-Nekhebet, and Hatshepsut-Meritre. Nevertheless, Thutmose most likely chose a son he had with a concubine named Isis as his successor.

Aged four or five at the king's death, this son was enthroned as Pharaoh Thutmose III. Because of his youth, Queen Hatshepsut carried out the regency. But she was not satisfied with the role of regent. Once installed on the throne she held on to it, even when Thutmose became old enough to reign, and wielded its power like an actual pharaoh until her death.

Even today, Hatshepsut's character is the object of passionate controversy. Some see her as a formidable usurper, authoritarian, scheming with her supporters to keep Thutmose III away from power. They see her as ambitious and more interested in retaining her power than protecting the interests of Egypt. For others, she comes across as a remarkable pharaoh, diplomatic and peace-loving, gifted with real political acumen. She certainly was a woman with an exceptional personality,

ambitious indeed, but who knew how to surround herself with dedicated and efficient functionaries, and who managed to keep peace in the Empire. Her reign was a period of prosperity and commercial and artistic expansion for Egypt. Her statues show a beautiful woman with a fine face, slender and youthful, with almond-shaped eyes.

Little by little, Hatshepsut transformed her regency into a kind of co-regency where she held the royal power herself, while Thutmose III, always represented at her side but ranking second, seems to have had the role of army chief. The fact remains that Thutmose was not entirely ousted, as it is often reported. During political and religious ceremonies, Hatshepsut and Thutmose III figured side by side. In the inscriptions, dynastic honors and glorifications are shared. Nevertheless, the reins of power were firmly in Hatshepsut's hands.

Why did Thutmose III, who would become one of the most glorious pharaohs and lead Egypt to its apogee, allow himself to be kept from power by a woman for so many years? The mystery remains unsolved. What conspiracies, what intrigues shook his entourage? The documentation available today does not yield any clues.

Hatshepsut's Temple at Deir el-Bahari

Sesenmut took inspiration from Mentuhotep's terraced temple, and next to it he built Queen Hatshepsut's "Temple of a Million Years," in the great rocky amphitheatre at Deir el-Bahari. The building rises elegantly at the foot of the cliff, and today one can still admire the lightness and purity of line of this architectural complex in white limestone.

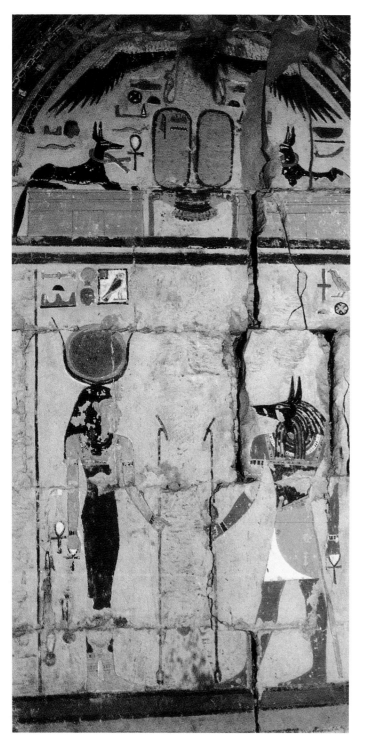

It was most likely in the seventh year of Thutmose III's reign that Hatshepsut was crowned and took the title of pharaoh.

Undoubtedly the crowning took place during "the Beautiful Feast of Opet."

This great yearly festival, presided by the king and the high Theban clergy, took place in the beginning of the second month of the Akhet season, when the Nile floods.

The sacred barque containing the statue of the god Amun-Re' left the temple at Karnak, born over the shoulders of thirty priests, followed by the barque of Mut, wife of Amun, and that of their son, Khonsu.

The three barques proceeded towards the Nile amidst the joyous crowd, accompanied by the hubbub of tambourines, trumpets, and sistrums, and the smoke of incense. They were then hoisted on board a vast boat, the userhat, whose stern and prow bore the head of a ram, Amun's sacred animal.

The boat rode the Nile up to Luxor, followed by the official cortège on boats and by the procession of the faithful walking along the riverbank.

The barques were unloaded in the midst of chants, dances, and pilgrims making offerings. They were taken to the temple at Luxor. There the sovereign and the priests celebrated the rites of Opet, which have remained a secret to this day.

The ceremonies lasted from ten to twenty days, during which the people caroused. Then the barques made their way back, in a procession that mirrored the arrival in every way, and the Theban triad re-entered its temple at Karnak.

Scenes from Hatshepsut's crowning decorate the walls of the Red Chapel, which the queen erected for Amun's barque. This chapel was restored in modern times.

The scenes depict Amun's procession, and include the following moments during the procession: the god issuing an oracle in favor of Hatshepsut, and the queen taking her place in the cortège; rites being celebrated in the temple at Karnak; the queen receiving Re's ornaments, the uraeus and the pschent (the double crown of Upper and Lower Egypt); and, once having become pharaoh, Hatshepsut removing the finery of the wife of Amun and passing this function to her daughter, Neferure.

To legitimise her throne, Hatshepsut invoked the authority of her father, Thutmose I. She engraved a text on the eighth pylon of the temple at Karnak, in which Thutmose I thanks the god Amun for having offered the throne of Egypt to his daughter Hatshepsut.

In a further effort to justify her ascent to the throne, Hatshepsut had scenes of a myth sculpted on the walls of her funerary temple at Deir el-Bahari.

The illustrations and text describe Hatshepsut's divine conception, her birth, and the announcement of her exceptional destiny. The concept of theogamy denotes a "divine" marriage between a god and the Great Royal Wife, future mother of the heir.

In the fifth dynasty, Sahure and Neferirkare Kakai took the title of "sons of Re'," conceived by the god Re' and the queen, establishing a precedent. In turn, Hatshepsut proclaimed herself daughter of the god Amun-Re' and of Ahmes, the Great Royal Wife of Thutmose I.

The texts explain how Amun took the appearance of the king to present himself to the queen, and how he disclosed his divine force to her in order to beget the child. Then Amun announced to Queen Ahmes that they had just conceived a daughter meant for an illustrious destiny, to be queen of Upper and Lower Egypt.

Thot, the messenger of the gods, announced the future birth. Khnum, the divine potter, Isis and Nephthys, Heket, and Meskhenet the goddess of labor, presided over the birth. Then Hathor presented the child to Amun and nursed her. Amun presented the child to all the gods. Later, Hatshepsut, having become a beautiful young woman, received the pharaohs' double crown from the hands of the gods before receiving it from the hands of men.

To establish her power and accomplish her works, Hatshepsut surrounded herself with zealous high functionaries, loyal beyond reproach. The two most powerful of these were Senenmut and Hapuseneb.

Favored by the queen, Senenmut was the dignitary closest to Hatshepsut, to whom he offered true devotion. He was already attached to the palace as chancellor of the House of Hatshepsut under Thutmose II. With Ahmose Pen-Nekhebet, he was also preceptor to Princess Neferure.

Senenmut was able to earn the confidence and favor of the queen, and he accumulated many duties, administrative as well as religious. He was: chief of the House of Amun, of its granary, its domains, its gardens, its herds; the servant priest of the userhat (Amun's barque); the priest of Maat; chief of the priests (servants) of Mentu at Hermonthis; overseer of all royal works; leader of festivals; and treasurer.

He was especially talented as overseer of works, directing the great building projects initiated by Hatshepsut. He is celebrated above all as the architect of the queen's magnificent funerary temple at Deir el-Bahari. He built a cenotaph and two tombs for himself, one of which was located at Deir el-Bahari. The image and the different names of the queen appear with great frequency on his monuments.

The other influential personage of the kingdom was Hapuseneb, who belonged to a family of priests. He was Hatshepsut's vizier and High Priest (First Servant) of Amun. To this high religious function he added that of "chief of all priests." He inspected all great works and supervised voyages.

There were some forty high dignitaries among the queen's faithful. Ahmose was vizier, either before Hapuseneb, or for the South. His son User was also vizier, and his grandson was Rekhmire, Thutmose III's famous vizier. Djehuty was royal treasurer. Senemiah was "royal scribe," chancellor of the treasury. Chancellor Nehesy directed the commercial expedition that the queen organised to the land of Punt.

Hatshepsut encouraged trade with Asia and expeditions to the mines of the Sinai. The most prestigious of her reign's commercial expeditions was to Punt, the details of which figure on the second portico at Deir el-Bahari. It was the god Amun who, through an oracle, elicited this trip, commanding his daughter Hatshepsut to send an army to Punt and seek incense trees.

The queen gave Senenmut and Nehesy her instructions for the organisation of this expedition.

After a long trip, the boats landed at Punt. Nehesy was welcomed by the leader of the country and his obese wife. The Egyptians brought gifts: collars and bracelets, pearls, weapons. In exchange, the leader of Punt offered

bags of incense and aromatic gums, spices, gold and electrum, ivory and ebony, and panther pelts to the royal envoy. The Egyptians collected many incense trees, but they also took monkeys, a giraffe, a leopard, and a panther back to Egypt. Some inhabitants of Punt joined the Egyptians for the return voyage.

The queen personally welcomed the travellers. The wonders of Punt were offered to Amun and enriched the treasure at Karnak. Hatshepsut erected many new monuments in Egypt. She sent an expedition to the Aswan quarries, where two obelisks were carved and then transported to Karnak. There they were covered in electrum and placed in Thutmose I's hypostyle hall, rising between the fourth and fifth pylons.

With Senenmut, the queen restored various monuments destroyed by the Hyksos. She rebuilt a stone temple to Pakhet, a lioness or cat goddess, that the Greeks would later name Speos Artemidos.

At Karnak, Hatshepsut built the Red Chapel, meant to house the barque of Amun. She erected a new pylon, the eighth.

At Elephantine she built a sandstone chapel, flanked by two obelisks, in honor of Khnum. She rebuilt the white limestone temple in Hermopolis dedicated to Thot and to the primordial Ogdoad composed of frog and serpent gods. She built a stone chapel at Ibrim, in Nubia, and a temple at Buhen in Horus' honor.

But Hatshepsut's most remarkable foundation is her funerary temple at Deir el-Bahari, Senenmut's masterpiece, which the Egyptians named "Djeser Djeseru," the "most magnificent of the magnificent," or the "most sublime of the sublimes."

A lane (the Greek "dromos") bordered with sphinxes bearing Hatshepsut's face used to lead from the valley temple today in ruins, to a pylon, now destroyed, opening onto a vast court.

This court was decorated with perseas, palm trees, and tamarisks; it was there that the incense trees brought over from Punt were replanted. Two ponds were also created at that site.

From this court, one can see the temple itself, composed of three terraces in storeys connected by ramps. The first ramp rises towards the lower terrace, containing two porticoes.

Thutmose III's Chapel

North of Mentuhotep's temple at Deir el-Bahari, there was a small chapel, built by Thutmose III, which has been transferred to the Egyptian Museum in Cairo. The mural painting in the back of the edifice shows a standing Thutmose III, dressed in royal finery. He is making an offering of water and incense to Amun, who is seated and wearing the high crown of the two feathers.

Deir el-Bahari

Perfectly adopting the forms of the western cliff, Hatshepsut's temple spreads over three successive terraces of harmonious proportions. There remains little of the third terrace, but its portico of columns, though damaged, retains its grand dimensions and majesty.

Hathor's chapel

South of the intermediate terrace of the funerary temple at Deir el-Bahari there is a three-chambered chapel dedicated to Hathor. Here the goddess is venerated in the form of a cow, as protectress of the city of the dead whose local cult is probably very ancient.

The back is decorated with bas-reliefs depicting the transport and the consecration of the obelisks carved at Aswan, and scenes of royal hunting and fishing.

The second terrace contains two porticoes with sculpted bas-reliefs illustrating, on the one side, the expedition to Punt, and, on the other side, the theogamy and birth of Hatshepsut. At the extremities there are two chapels cut into the rocky cliff.

One of them, with a hypostyle hall, is dedicated to Anubis. The other is consecrated to Hathor, the celestial wet nurse, and it contains two hypostyle halls. Hathoric pillars bearing the goddess' head with cow's ears adorn the first one.

This chapel to Hathor, the goddess of life, love, and joy, and, as lady of the necropolis, of death, became the arrival point of Amun's barque during the Festival of the Valley.

Each year, on the occasion of this feast, the god Amun, accompanied by the pharaoh, crossed the Nile on the userhat in a procession and visited the gods of the West and the deceased who were buried there. Rites of regeneration were then performed, waking the spirits of the dead. The living communed joyfully with their dead and feasted on the burial grounds.

A portico with Hatshepsut's Osirian pillars, flanked by a hypostyle hall and two chapels, rises from the third terrace. The sanctuary, cut into the rock, contains three halls surrounded by niches.

Hatshepsut built two tombs for herself. The first, unfinished, was cut into a cliff located between the Valley of the Kings and the Valley of the Queens, when the sovereign was still Great Royal Wife. It contained her first sarcophagus, in yellow quartzite. However, as soon as Hatshepsut became pharaoh, she abandoned these efforts and undertook the construction of a second tomb, situated this time in the Valley of the Kings, cut in the other side of the cliff that overhangs her funerary temple. Two sarcophagi, one of which had been transformed to receive Thutmose I, were found there.

The illustrious Thutmose III

Thutmose truly rose to power at around age thirty, on the twenty-second year of his own reign (he attributed Hatshepsut's years of reign to himself).

He who had thus far remained in his aunt's shadow became a great pharaoh, undoubtedly the greatest in Egyptian history. He reigned thirty more years at the head of an immense empire with Thebes as its capital.

Thutmose was most importantly a prestigious conqueror, a brave war chief and a fine strategist who led his army from victory to victory. He led a campaign in Asia, where a coalition of Syrian princes clustered around the prince of Kadesh, a city on the Oronte river north of the Retenu region.

This region of Retenu and Canaan (Syro-Palestine) was composed of principalities, buffer states between Egypt and the recent kingdom of Mitanni, on the Upper Euphrates, a kingdom motivated by the thirst for conquest.

Thutmose III needed four expeditions to get the better of this coalition and four more to impose his power on the Phoenician cities, defeat the Mitanni, and push them beyond the Euphrates, thereby re-establishing Thutmose I's frontier.

The sovereign demonstrated his tactical intelligence in the taking of Meggido, his first strategic objective. After the fall of Meggido, Thutmose continued his victorious march northwards, conquering the whole of Retenu and the Phoenician ports. In each city he put a new chief in power, while making sure to preserve the local governments.

The king immortalised his triumph by inscribing, on the sixth and seventh pylons of Amun's temple at Karnak, the names of the subjugated peoples.

Afterwards Thutmose III led two campaigns to achieve control in Asia. At the end of the second campaign, he had bas-reliefs sculpted depicting the flora of Retenu in a group of halls in Karnak that today are called the "Botanical Gardens."

Then, after having ensured his hegemony over the Phoenician ports, he sacked Kadesh. The children of local princes were taken as hostages to Egypt, where they were educated according to Egyptian mores. Thus Egyptianised, they were meant to return to their countries and propagate the victor's culture.

The sovereign then prepared for the campaign against the Mitanni. His carefully thought-out strategy ensured victory. He had boats built at Byblos, which he took across the desert on bull-drawn chariots all the way to the Euphrates. These boats allowed the Egyptian army to cross the Euphrates and beat the Mitanni on the other riverbank. Thutmose thus established this natural frontier as the limit of his empire, blocking the expansion of the Mitanni's ambitions.

Henceforth, Thutmose III led a yearly campaign in Asia to supervise the conquered lands and to repress local revolts. His last expedition was to defeat a new coalition that had formed around the prince of Tunip.

In Nubia, the sovereign led a single campaign to repress a Sudanese revolt.

Thutmose III was the undisputed master of an immense empire stretching from the Euphrates in the north, to the Nile's fourth cataract in the south. The pharaoh-god reigned over a group of countries federated around Egypt, where each country was politically autonomous.

The king was a valiant hero, the "Sun of Nine Arcs." He drew his greatness and his force from Amun-Re', whom he consulted before departing for each campaign. At Karnak, he erected a stele on which the god Amun reveals to the pharaoh, in a veritable victorious hymn, the extent of his power over the foreign countries and the subjugated peoples. He offers him all the lands, from north to south and from east to west, and procures for him the force to maintain his omnipotence.

The abundant booty flowing from all these campaigns brought multiple riches to Egypt, most of which were consecrated to Amun's domain.

Thutmose III's Annals, a long text on the walls of a hall in Karnak, relates the pharaoh's campaigns and details the booty earned by each victory.

The Meggido booty, for instance, was composed of weapons, precious objects, precious crockery and furniture, gold, horses, herds, produce, prisoners, women, children, and servants.

The itemization of it all is precisely kept. The booty from Retenu was rich in grains, olive oil, wines, fruit, incense, and honey.

Besides the booty that the army brought over from each campaign, Egypt collected an annual tribute from each subjugated country, according to the country's own wealth.

Retenu, a very rich country, sent fruits, honey, wine, oil, cattle, asses, horses, silver, copper and tin, precious stones, arms, chariots, and precious objects. Phoenicia gave wheat, oil, cattle, asses, horses, copper, and tin.

From Africa came gold, ivory, and ebony. Retenu and Africa even sent servants and women with dowries for the pharaoh's harem. Egypt also imposed military service on the subjugated states. All states, but most especially Phoenicia and its fleet, were required to participate in war operations.

Besides this tribute from vanquished states, there were also tributes that certain other states sent to Egypt willingly as proof of friendship. Cyprus sent copper; Assyria, lapis-lazuli; Hatti, precious stones; Punt, incense and myrrh. These tributes enriched the House of Amun.

This incredible abundance turned Egypt into a great economic power. To further encourage commercial development, Thutmose III undertook initiatives to create a sea port south of the island of Pharos, near the coast. (This would later be continued by Ramesses II.)

All Aegean and Phoenician vessels trading with Egypt passed through this point. It was Thutmose III who first understood the significance of this location, which later became Alexandria.

This prosperous empire relied on a powerful administration. Like his illustrious stepmother, Thutmose III was clever enough to surround himself with competent and faithful high functionaries.

On the walls of their tomb at Sheikh Abd el Gurnah, the vizier User and his nephew and successor Rekhmire (wise like Re') left texts detailing their installation into office and the many duties and responsibilities of the vizier. Rekhmire's tomb contains magnificent paintings that show the vizier fulfilling his functions, receiving people's petitions, receiving tributes, collecting taxes, inspecting shops.

Thutmose III's heraldic pillars at Karnak

The dualism enhancing the formal opposition between Lower and Upper Egypt remains one of the fundamental notions of pharaonic civilisation. Thus the "Double Land" or "Country of Two Lands" – that is, unified Egypt – is often symbolised by the image of Upper Egypt's lotus facing Lower Egypt's papyrus.

He was also shown at leisure, savoring nature, hunting, fishing, and music.

The highest religious dignitary was the High Priest of Amun, Mekhenperrasenb, who was very close to Thutmose III. The Second Servant of Amun, Puyemre, was also a talented architect. He served both under Hatshepsut and Thutmose III.

Min, the High Priest of Osiris and Onuris (warrior god assimilated by Thot, Onuris held Hathor back when she became the Eye of Re' and threatened to destroy humanity) was chancellor of Lower Egypt and preceptor of the future Amenhotep II.

Amenenhab, the courageous chief of the archers, was an intimate of the sovereign, and most likely a childhood friend. He was a "child of the Kep," a royal institution that belonged to the Palace where the princes and young nobles were educated.

The children of foreign princes that were taken as hostages to Egypt were also raised there. The "children of the Kep" who chose a military career were among the king's best officers. Amenenhab accompanied Thutmose III in all his campaigns. His career continued under Amenhotep II.

Another military man, General Thaneni, was the army's scribe. The important task of keeping an account of royal campaigns fell to him.

The glory of having taken Joppe (Jaffa) belongs to General Dhouti. A legendary account has survived through a tale written during the 19th dynasty. According to this tale, General Dhouti, who did not succeed in taking the city by force, invited the prince of Joppe to feast outside the city, made him drunk, and killed him, using King Menkheperre's (Thutmose III's) mace. Then Dhouti brought two hundred baskets, in which as many soldiers hid.

The driver of the prince's chariot, who was waiting nearby, was told that the prince had captured Dhouti, together with his wife and children, and secured them in the baskets. The driver of the chariot was then told that the prince ordered him to take the captives to Joppe. Two hundred Egyptian soldiers were thus able to penetrate the city and open its gates to the rest of the army, and Joppe fell.

A conqueror and builder in the tradition of the pharaohs of the 18th dynasty, Thutmose III was among the Egyptian sovereigns who made the most significant contributions to the splendor of Amun's great temple at Karnak. He erected two new pylons, the sixth and seventh, providing them with a gate in pink granite. The seventh pylon bears his depiction as vanquisher of the Asians and a list of the subjugated peoples.

Two colossal statues of the king and two obelisks in pink granite adorn the pylon. Six colossi in limestone and pink quartzite were also erected in front of Hatshepsut's pylon (the eighth). Bas-reliefs were sculpted on the sixth pylon, illustrating the Meggido victory.

The text of the Annals, relating Thutmose III's campaigns, figures in the U-shaped corridor that surrounds the naos.

The sovereign finished Thutmose's hypostyle hall, located between the fourth and fifth pylons.

In annexed halls, he depicted exotic animals and plants gathered during an expedition to Retenu. These halls constitute the famous "Botanical Gardens."

Next to it, Thutmose III built the Akhmenu sanctuary, the "brilliant monument" where rites of regeneration – through which the king received the renewal of his divine force from Amun – took place.

In the center of this temple stands a great hall, the "Hall of Festivals," with columns bearing texts of praise delivered to the king by the gods. Annexes were dedicated to Sokaris, the ancient god of the Memphite necropolis.

Thutmose III built another sanctuary outside Amun's temple. It contained a hall with six Osirian pillars and a naos with an enthroned statue of Amun and another of the sovereign. At Karnak, the king also restored a temple dedicated to Ptah.

Outside Karnak, his name remains connected with numerous monuments, notably a chapel to Amun at Elephantine and temples in Nubia consecrated to Horus, Dedun, and Khnum.

Thutmose III's tomb was constructed in the Valley of the Kings. The *Book of Amduat* figures on its walls. An empty sarcophagus in red sandstone was found in the tomb; the mummy was found at the hiding place in Deir el-Bahari.

The great sovereign had two Great Royal Wives, one of whom was Hatshepsut-Meritre, daughter of Hatshepsut and Thutmose II. She gave Thutmose III dynastic legitimacy and an heir, Amenhotep III, who was co-regent for three years before succeeding his father.

Pages 76-77:
Luxor

Serving as temple of the New Year at Karnak, Luxor was used for the voyage of the god Amun during the rites performed to celebrate the New Year. Built essentially by Amenhotep III and Ramesses II, this architectural complex is rather more modest than the one at Karnak. Amenhotep III's court is bordered by porticos with columns in the form of fascicles that are topped with closed, papyrus-shaped capitals.

The merciless Amenhotep II

Amenhotep II was eighteen years old when he ascended to the throne. Until then, he had been a priest in Memphis. He was an athletic young man. It was said that he was strong and tireless. A stele found buried near the Giza Sphinx stresses the youth's beauty and physical force, presenting him as an invincible archer, a peerless equestrian who loved horses and knew how to train them, an unbeatable runner and indefatigable rower. He is depicted as a veritable hero, powerful and courageous, whose superhuman force manifested itself in athletic or soldierly exploits.

Amenhotep II waged two campaigns in Asia to maintain his father's conquests. During the first one, he advanced in a quick march to Retenu and Naharina, all the way to the Euphrates.

He vanquished a coalition of Syrian princes from the Takhsy region, between the Oronte and the Euphrates. He appears to have been rather brutal, killing the seven chiefs with mace blows delivered by his own hand, and then hanging the men in front of Thebes' high walls as an example.

The second expedition in Asia was apparently aimed at subduing another coalition of rebellious Syrians. The repression was horrible. Amenhotep II threw the prisoners into two ditches and set fire to them. The pharaoh personally supervised their agony. Such cruelty towards the vanquished enemy has no parallel in Egyptian history.

Powerful functionaries gravitated around the king. They included Usir-Sater, governor of the South, friend of the king and his companion in arms; Sennefer, the mayor of Thebes and manager of the harem; Kenamun, the king's foster-brother, a great financier and overseer of festivities, whose tomb contains delicate paintings announcing the artistic evolution that would rise under Amenhotep III; the High Priest Mekhenperrasenb, still in charge; and his successors Meri and Amenemhet.

The eighth pylon at Karnak

The temple to Amun at Karnak has two main axes. In the east/west direction, there is a succession of six pylons (numbered from one to six). Then, at the height of the fourth pylon, a transversal axis running north/south towards the temple of Mut has four pylons (numbered from seven to ten). Here we are in front of the southern face of the eighth pylon, built by Hatshepsut. The decor, which was executed by Amenhotep II, represents the king massacring his enemies.

The latter left some *Instructions to his children*, a classic genre of the time, in his tomb.

Amenhotep II built a chapel between the ninth and tenth pylons at Karnak. He erected columns of white sandstone and gold in the hypostyle hall built by Thutmose I and Thutmose III between the fourth and fifth pylons. On the eighth pylon, he depicted himself massacring enemies with mace blows. He erected two obelisks. He finished the construction of buildings undertook by Thutmose III at El-Kab, sanctuaries that are dedicated to Thot and Nekhbet.

His tomb in the Valley of the Kings comprises a large hall with green walls, symbolic of the vegetation cycle, and bearing the text of the *Book of Amduat*. The royal mummy was found in its red sarcophagus, covered with flowers.

The peaceful Thutmose IV

Thutmose IV, his successor, was the son of Amenhotep II and Tiaa, the Great Royal Wife. His ascent to the throne had been predicted by the Giza Sphinx, which represented the god Re'-Horakhty, or Harmakhis (Re'-Horus of the Horizon). While hunting in the desert, the young prince rested near the Sphinx, at that time deeply buried in sand, and fell asleep.

The god came to him in a dream and announced that, in exchange for his promise to free the Sphinx from the sand, he would be made king one day. Thutmose IV agreed, and once he became king, he had the Sphinx uncovered. Then he erected a stele relating the dream episode.

The new pharaoh applied himself to keeping the peace and stability of the empire. His expedition to the South was a triumphant march and a prestigious operation. The tributes kept arriving from all over. Thutmose IV's wedding to King Artatama's daughter, who became Great Royal Wife, advanced an alliance with the Mitanni. The pharaoh also made an alliance with Babylon.

At Karnak, Thutmose IV built an alabaster sanctuary for the barque of Amun, and a large building in sandstone, today rather ruined. Some of its blocks were discovered in the foundations of Amenhotep III's third pylon.

*Located beyond the third pylon
of the temple to Amun at
Karnak, in a section where the
structures are rather complex,
Amenhotep III's scarab-beetle is
surprisingly original. An
enormous scarab-beetle sits
prominently on a high pedestal
engraved with scenes of the king
making offerings to the god
Atum-Khepri. The obelisks of
Hatshepsut and Thutmose I
appear in the distance.*

The king had the gate of the fourth pylon enlarged, and built a golden porch in front of the pylon.

He was in his thirties when he died. His mummy was found in Amenhotep II's tomb.

The diplomatic Amenhotep III

Amenhotep III was the son of Thutmose IV and his Great Royal Wife, the Mitanni princess whose Egyptian name was Mutemwiya. Amenhotep III succeeded his father around 1408 BC.

He proclaimed himself son of Amun-Re', and depicted the scenes of the divine conception and birth on the walls of the temple to Amun he erected at Luxor.

Amenhotep III, who through his mother was half-Mittani in origin, was a true Oriental potentate: diplomatic, refined, indolent, and lavish.

Under his reign, the splendor of Thebes was unequalled. Thebes, with its multiple architectural beauties, was a prosperous capital of a powerful empire. It was a noisy and cosmopolitan city, and a great trading port on the river. The Greeks called it "the city of a hundred gates," alluding to its pylons and temples.

Ever since Amenhotep I, all the pharaohs strove to make the capital a city of extraordinary wealth and splendor, the most opulent in Antiquity, but it was under the reign of Amenhotep III that it achieved its apogee. The king contributed much to improving Thebes, notably with the construction of the Luxor temple. His reign was a period of evolution for Egyptian civilisation, enriched by his Asian influence.

It was also a period of peace. Amenhotep III did not launch into great military expeditions the way his ancestors did; there was a single campaign, in Nubia. This pharaoh was not a warrior.

He continued the era of diplomacy that had already been initiated under Thutmose IV. Egypt already possessed a considerable empire.

Instead of further attempting to spread its conquests, it applied itself to preserving friendly relations with Mitanni and to furthering commercial relations with Asia and Africa.

The king kept up a political correspondence with the Asian states and the Phoenician princes. At his ascent he sent an ambassador to his uncle Shuttarna II, to confirm the alliance with Mittani. Amenhotep III reinforced the alliances by marrying Asian princesses. He married his cousin Gilakhipa, sister of Tushratta (the new Mittani sovereign).

He also married first the sister, then the daughter of the king of Babylon.

The temple in Luxor

*Though somewhat destroyed,
the façade at Luxor shows the
different elements that formed a
temple entrance in ancient
Egypt: two obelisks (the one on
the right is now at the Place de
la Concorde in Paris), six
colossal statues (of which
three, representing Ramesses II
standing, have disappeared),
and the pylon with two
trapezoid towers. The four
grooves visible here once held
wooden masts with flags.*

But he refused to give his own daughter in marriage to the king of Babylon in return, which greatly insulted the Babylonian king.

Commercial treaties were concluded with Cyprus. A substantial wood and copper allocation was allowed into Egypt, and Cyprus was given an exemption from customs taxes.

Of all of Amenhotep III's wives and the many women of his harem, his favorite was the Great Royal Wife, Tiy, who came from a modest, possibly sacerdotal, background.

Her parents, Yuya and Tuya, were bestowed with honors by the king. At the occasion of his marriage to Tiy, the king issued a series of scarabs bearing the announcement of the event, which were sent throughout the empire.

Memnon's Colossi

Memnon's Colossi are the sole remnants of Amenhotep III's funerary temple. In Antiquity they were the object of a legend. One of them, partially destroyed, supposedly emitted a musical vibration at sunrise. The sound was attributed to the Ethiopian Memnon. Killed by Achilles in the Trojan war, he was said to be moaning in pain. But the Roman Emperor Septimus Severus restored the statue, which afterwards became silent.

Similarly, he distributed series of scarabs for all his outstanding actions. Amenhotep imposed his choice in a brilliant manner, treating his wife with consideration and showering her with favors. He dug a large pleasure lake for her. He associated her closely with the political direction of the country.

In effect Tiy played an eminent role in the affairs of Egypt, particularly in diplomacy, where she constantly advised the king.

She was a great queen, influential, elegant, and refined. She started the fashion of pleated clothes and plaited wigs that framed the bust.

She preferred the new aesthetics where hieratic conventions were giving way to fine features and delicacy.

The union of Amenhotep III and Tiy begat Amenhotep IV and five daughters. The king married one of these daughters, Sitamun, and gave her the equivalent status of Great Royal Wife.

At Malgatta, near Medinet Habu on the west bank of the Thebes, the sovereign built a residence containing four palaces, one of which was for Queen Tiy, and a temple to Amun. Many official ceremonies took place there, including Amenhotep III's jubilees, or Sed festivals. In principle, a jubilee took place once every thirty years of a pharaoh's reign, but certain pharaohs celebrated a second, and even a third, not long after the first one. The ceremony's rites renewed the royal powers. Its significance was both political and religious.

One of the most eminent characters in the king's entourage was Amenhotep, son of Hapu. Originally from Athribis, in the Delta, this man started his career as scribe. He was initiated into ritual writings. Then the king attached him as royal scribe, and put him in charge of educating young military men and of managing the military personnel. He organised the system of defence in the Delta frontiers so efficiently that the king, very satisfied with his services, named him overseer of all royal works.

He quickly acquired great influence in the affairs of the country, equalling and even surpassing the vizier. He had the reputation of a wise master. The king granted him the right to build a funerary temple for himself, a privilege normally reserved for the royal family. Amenhotep was divinised. It was believed that he had the power of healing and the gift of issuing oracles.

If Amenhotep, son of Hapu was the most powerful royal dignitary, the vizier Ramose was the most superb. His tomb and Khaemhat's are among the most beautiful at Gurnah. On the walls are bas-reliefs rendered with very delicate lines highlighting the elegance of the finery.

Khaemhat, superintendent of the granary of Upper and Lower Egypt, was a very cultivated man. His tomb contains several tableaux depicting him while fulfilling his functions, as well as mystical scenes and beautiful religious texts.

Ptahmose accumulated the charges of High Priest of Amun and vizier of the South.

Amenhotep III was a great builder, but in erecting his monuments he thought nothing of demolishing those of his predecessors and using the blocks for himself.

**Apuya,
Ramose's mother**

*The southeast wall of Ramose's
tomb in Thebes depicts the
funerary festivities. This detail
represents Ramose's mother,
Apuya, "the gods' beloved,"
and shows the apogee of the art
of bas-relief in the New
Kingdom. All the details of the
hairstyle, the jewellery, and the
face are indicated with
remarkable precision on the fine
limestone of the walls.*

To build the third pylon of the temple at Karnak, for instance, he used pillars from a construction of Thutmose III's located next to the fourth pylon (constructed by Thutmose I). In the foundations of the third pylon, blocks were found that came from various monuments from Thutmose IV and Amenhotep II. In addition, he used blocks from Amenhotep I's alabaster chapel and Senusret I's White Chapel, but both buildings have since been entirely reconstructed.

The king also built a temple consecrated to Mentu. Today it is in ruins, but it was once considered splendid due to its rich materials. South of the temple to Amun, he erected a temple to the god's companion, Mut. The temple contained several black granite statues of the lioness goddess Sekhmet.

At Luxor, Amenhotep III destroyed the existing temple, which dated from the 12th dynasty, and re-used its blocks to erect a new temple. Luxor, the "southern harem of Amun," which the god attended as a visitor during the Feast of Opet, was henceforth an elegant construction with slender colonnades. The temple had two naos. One was the barque sanctuary, and the other contained the god's statue. The famous hall of the royal birth was at Luxor. Under a court in the temple, five perfectly preserved statues were recently unearthed. One, in pink quartzite, was of Amenhotep III, another

of Tiy in black granite, another of Hathor and Horemheb (who became Akhenaten's general and later pharaoh) adoring the god Atum. Amenhotep III erected chapels at El-Kab and Elephantine and temples in Nubia, notably at Soleb, between the second and third cataracts.

The sovereign built himself a funerary temple in the Valley of the Kings, of which only two royal colossi remain, the famous Colossi of Memnon. Amenhotep III set his tomb in the Valley of the Monkeys, named after the fact that it used to have a necropolis of sacred monkeys.

A religious evolution began under Amenhotep III that would eventually lead to Akhenaton's Amarnian episode.

The reign's end is marked by a degradation of international politics. Asia swarmed with intrigues. Faced with the new power of the Hittites, the Mittani weakened; the Hittite King Suppiluliuma attacked Egypt's allies, the Mittani princes of Syria. Amenhotep III did not intervene, despite the Syrian princes' pleas for help. Egypt signed a treaty with the Hittites. The prince of Kadesh and the king of Amurru plotted to form coalitions of small states; this too the pharaoh ignored. Upon his death, Amenhotep III bequeathed his son, Amenhotep IV, an empire where disorder was growing. Under the reign of the new pharaoh, the empire would deteriorate even more.

Pages 84-85:
Ramose's mourners

*This is one of the most
celebrated scenes of Egyptian
mural painting. It is from
Ramose's tomb at Gurnah.
Ramose was governor of Thebes
under Amenhotep III. Here,
the funeral cortège, followed by
professional mourners performing
gestures of lamentation, seems
to advance with a slowness that
enhances the ceremony's
solemnity.*

THE AMARNA PERIOD TUTANKHAMUN

The mystic pharaoh: Akhenaten

Upon Amenhotep III's death, the immense Theban empire was being threatened from all sides. Nevertheless, riches continued to flow to the capital and to the god of Thebes, Amun. His clergy were at the top of their power. The new pharaoh, Amenhotep IV, would turn away from the interests of the state and the official religion to dedicate himself to his mystical ideal, centered on the god Aten. This era, which remains obscure and impenetrable, is called the Amarna Period.

Amenhotep IV rose to the throne around 1370 BC at the young age of roughly fifteen. Some believe he was co-regent for three years, during which his father Amenhotep III was rather aged and ill. It is speculated that the reins of power were held by the Great Royal Wife and the prince's mother, Tiy. Some historians contest the regency, while others assign it a much greater length.

The Amarna Reform

From the time he took the throne, the young Amenhotep IV started to set up a veritable monotheistic religious reform in favor of Aten, at first discreetly, and then in an ever more radical manner.

This reform aimed to promote Aten from how he had been perceived thus far (as the merely physical manifestation of Re' made visible to all, the solar disk) to the one and only god who was light and the very source of life itself.

The seed for this new interpretation of Aten had already been planted under Amenhotep III, probably with the encouragement of Queen Tiy. The palace of Malgatta had been named "Aten's Splendor" by

Amenhotep III, almost certainly influenced by the Great Royal Wife, whose pleasure boat also bore that name. It may be assumed, then, that it was Tiy who instilled in Amenhotep IV this new religious thinking that he would promote as an all-powerful ideal, at least for the court and for the duration of his reign.

The young king's fervor for Aten went hand in hand with his awareness of the excessive political influence of Amun's high clergy, who continued to accumulate religious functions and political and administrative duties. To diminish the high priest's power, the new pharaoh stripped him of his function as administrator of Amun's riches. Likewise, he rebelled against the priests of Amun's wealth and against the rites of the traditional religion, which seemed to him idolatrous, empty of meaning, and not conducive to bringing the people closer to their god.

The idealistic sovereign believed in the equality of men at birth, and the kinship of all living creatures. He wanted to demystify and simplify the cult, in order to make it accessible to all. At Karnak he erected a temple to Aten, called *Gem Aten* (*Aten is found*), constituted of small blocks of sandstone or talatat that allowed for a much faster construction than those of the traditional temples composed of gigantic blocks.

Nevertheless, the pharaoh undoubtedly had to battle the hostility of Amun's clergy, who did not appreciate his reforms and the new importance accorded to Aten. So he hardened his position, rejected the other gods altogether, and changed his title. In the fourth year of his reign, he abandoned his name of Amenhotep, "Amun is satisfied," to take that of Akhenaten, "Servant of Aten." This was an essential step for him to take, because to the Egyptians, a person's name defined him. A pharaoh's name expressed his true nature. Its meaning was sacred and revealed his immortal being.

Nefertiti

Discovered in a dwelling at Tell el-Amarna, Nefertiti's unfinished head underlines yet again the fascinating beauty and nobility of Amenhotep IV's wife. The chisel's lines, still visible, and the outlines of black paint on the eyelashes, the eyes, and the forehead give this face a nearly unreal majesty and a bewitching grace.

Professing the sovereignty of his solar god, the king assigned him the name of "Re'-Horakhty," the Horus of the Horizon, and he became the solar disk worshipped in the Amarna cult.

Relief from Tell el-Amarna

Many sculptor's studies have been discovered at Tell el-Amarna, a city built and abandoned in less than thirty years. Here, this draft presents two royal personages (both wear the uraeus, the ultimate royal symbol). It probably represents Akhenaten and his successor, Smenkhkare, a pharaoh whose very existence remains hypothetical.

Akhenaten decided to settle in a new capital with his wife Nefertiti, who was also dedicated to the cult of Aten. Queen Nefertiti, "the beautiful one has come," is today the most celebrated of Egyptian women. The superb busts found at Amarna reveal the firm beauty of her face, which has been called "a miracle of balance." She was passionately loved by Akhenaten, who composed a love poem for her, inscribed on a stele, immortalising her as an ideal queen. This most beautiful of sovereigns, however, is also one of the most mysterious. Her origin is unknown, giving rise to various suppositions.

Some believe she was the daughter of Tushratta, King of Mittani, cousin of Amenhotep III. It was also believed for a while that she was the daughter of Ay, chief of the chariots, then Akhenaten's minister. Ay would later become vizier under Tutankhamun and even pharaoh during the turbulent end of the 18th dynasty. The fact that he carried the title of "Divine Father" underscored this speculation. But the hypothesis was abandoned when it was discovered that Ay's title was in reference to his wife, Tey, the queen's nurse. It is possible that Nefertiti was simply one of Amenhotep III's daughters, but this cannot be confirmed with certainty.

The royal couple decided to leave Thebes. The sovereign conceived a new city, consecrated to Aten, which he built from the ground up. For his capital, he chose an empty site near Hermopolis. He erected fourteen stelae to delimit the space where, over time,

palaces, houses, and temples dedicated to Aten and surrounded by gardens were built. The contemporary name of the site, Tell el-Amarna, is the origin of the terms "Amarna Period," "Amarna Reform," and even "Amarna Heresy" which refer to Akhenaten's reign. The pharaoh named his city Akhetaten, "Aten's horizon," and resolved never to shrink the city limits that he had fixed. In his reign's sixth year, the royal couple settled in the new capital with the princesses, Tiy, the Queen Mother, the court, and the government headed by the vizier Ramose, a supporter of the Atenian ideal. It was there that the cult of Aten (of whom the pharaoh considered himself the earthly manifestation) flourished.

Akhenaten has often been accused of making a total break with the established Egyptian religion, and has even been called a heretic. In fact, the idea of divine oneness was not new. Each god, to his faithful, was unique in his own way, each local divinity was a particular form of the divine. The Egyptian mentality was well able to conceive of oneness within multiplicity. Akhenaten's originality was expressed by his intolerance regarding the cult of Amun. Once installed at Amarna, the pharaoh ordered Aten's name to be chiselled onto all monuments throughout Egypt and even throughout the whole empire. He also ordered the suppression of the other gods' names, and forbade the word "god" to be used in the plural. As the most powerful god of Thebes, Amun was the main target, but the other gods were also persecuted. Many temples were closed, their riches confiscated and taken to Amarna.

To found the new cult, the sovereign took inspiration from the Heliopolitan tradition. He kept the name of Re'-Horakhty, *Re', Horus of the Horizon*, "who is in the disk," to designate his god. He kept the symbolism of the benben stone and the bull Mnevis, privileged settings where the solar god could be incarnated. He even borrowed the name of the High Priest of Heliopolis, *The Greatest of the Seers*, and attributed it to Meryre, High Priest of Aten. Finally, he built open-air temples to Aten, like those consecrated to Re' by the sovereigns of the fifth dynasty. But Akhenaten also simplified the solar myth, retaining only its diurnal aspect, Re'-Horakhty-Aten, and hiding its nocturnal element represented by Osiris, god of the dead, and complementary to Re'.

The new capital: Tell el-Amarna

The city of Akhetaten spread over the eastern bank of the Nile, in an area about fifteen kilometers (nine miles) long and six to eight kilometers (four to nine miles) wide. It was enclosed by a circle of limestone cliffs and delimited by Akhenaten's fourteen stelae, which depicted the royal family worshipping Aten.

The great temple to Aten was situated in the center of the city, and was entirely open to sunlight. Its floor plan was rectangular. Beyond the entrance pylon were a series of courts separated by porticoes. In these courts stood tables spread with offerings. The last court was the sanctuary, where the pharaoh met the god.

To the east, the temple was flanked by a smaller building, bearing the king's Osirian colossi, most likely devoted to the cult of Akhenaten, intimately connected with the cult of Aten. A little farther there was a second, smaller open-air temple dedicated to Aten, named *Aten's Castle.*

The center of the new capital also housed the palace and the official administration buildings. The great royal palace was composed of an immense court bordered by statues of the king and queen, an official home, several secondary courts with porticos, and a hypostyle reception hall.

The walls and floors boasted delicate paintings of floral motifs, or of fish and birds frolicking in the marshes. The king's house included a balcony where the pharaoh appeared in public, next to the queen and princesses. One of these occasions was the rewarding of gold (collars, cups, crockery) to the king's favorites, such as Ay, the "Divine Father." The sovereign's private residence was connected to the official palace by a gallery spanning the street.

The northern section of the city housed the merchants' neighborhood, as well as a pleasure palace with vast gardens containing a lake and a zoo populated by antelopes.

A summer palace was located in the southern section of Akhetaten. Its columns were inlaid with colored lotus-shaped motifs and its immense gardens, with their many ponds and artificial lakes, provided a respite from the heat. The houses of high functionaries, such as the one belonging to the vizier Nakht (Ramose's successor), were also found in this neighborhood.

These homes contained terraces, verdant gardens with ponds where fish swam amidst the lotus, and vast apartments.

Nearby were rows of the best artists' workshops, such as the sculptor Thutmes, whose favorite model was Nefertiti; his magnificent polychromatic bust, now in the Egyptian Museum in Berlin, made the queen's graceful face world-famous.

Akhenaten's necropolis was situated east of the city. The tombs were cut into the cliff. Akhenaten prepared a hypogeum for himself. However, he was never to occupy it.

Akhenaten as sphinx

For the first time, Egyptians worshipped a god without an image or statues. Aten, the ultimate principle of creation, is symbolised by a solar disk emitting light rays ending in hands. Here, the king is represented as a sphinx. The sun rays nearest his face hold the ankh (the cross of life).

The Amarna stele

This stele comes from a railing in the temple to Aten at Tell el-Amarna. The scene's iconography represents the new norm under Amenhotep IV's rule. It shows Akhenaten, wearing the crown of Upper Egypt, and Nefertiti offering ritual vases to Aten. The solar disk casts its rays down on the royal family.

It is in the artistic domain that the Amarna Revival had its greatest impact. It reflected the importance Akhenaten accorded to truth and the rhythms of real life, in harmony with his conception of the notion of Maat. The sovereign interpreted Maat not only as divine justice and order, but also as truth and even as the breath of life, symbolised in her aspect as Re's daughter. The solar god was the provider of life. Aten, the solar disk, was visible everywhere in Amarna. On the stelae delimiting the city, the solar disk is depicted casting down rays terminating in hands that offer the cross of life (the ankh) to the pharaoh, the queen, and the princesses.

Hereafter, naturalism in art was the rule. The artists busied themselves to represent the king in his familial intimacy. Bas-reliefs show us Akhenaten and Nefertiti feasting, drinking, and eating, all very uncommon subjects in the conventional scenes where one hardly ever saw royals bringing food to their mouths.

Amarna art also brought radical innovations in the renderings of portraits and statues of the sovereigns. Akhenaten was depicted with a caricatured, androgynous morphology: narrow shoulders, salient chest, wide hips, and swollen stomach. His head was exaggeratedly elongated, his face emaciated, with thick lips and a protruding chin. This strange iconography, which for a long time was seen as proof of the "mystic" pharaoh's abnormality or even madness, apparently did not correspond to his actual physique.

Most likely this unusual style of excessive representation had a symbolic meaning. If the pharaoh was to be depicted as the earthly manifestation of Aten, Aten's asexual nature had to be captured.

The pharaoh had to be depicted as the very incarnation of life-bestowing divine light, the sun being both mother and father to humans.

This new type of figuration quickly became the norm, and spread to the queen and the princesses, and finally to all other personages.

The cult was transformed, because it was essentially reduced to the cult of Aten and his earthly manifestation, Akhenaten, the veritable spiritual master of his people. The pharaoh and his close relatives attended the temple under an open sky every morning. Inundated with the sun's divine rays, the king and the priests consecrated the offerings in the courtyard. Everyone prayed together, raising their hands heavenwards to give grace to the benevolent god and to offer him flowers, fruits, and produce, the bounty of nature's perfection created by Aten.

The cult was free of obscurity and no longer confined the mystery of divine presence to the naos, the closed sanctuary of the traditional temples. All the faithful could watch this ceremony and unite their prayers to those of the priests and the king. Even though Akhenaten considered himself the privileged interlocutor of Aten, the intermediary between the god and men, he still attributed the title of High Priest to Meryre, the "beloved of Re'," who was also treasurer and superintendent of the harem.

The bas-reliefs and their accompanying texts in Meryre's tomb in Amarna recount the nomination ceremony where he was named High Priest of Aten by the god himself.

In other court members' tombs, famous Amarna Era hymns poetically and passionately exalt both Aten and the sovereign.

The failure of Amarna

Unfortunately, the mystic king devoted his life only to his god. The empire's administration and preservation didn't seem to interest him. The direction of the administration was trusted to the faithful of Aten. Tribute was still collected in Amarna.

The king, equally unconcerned with foreign politics, allowed the empire to disintegrate. The Hittite King Suppiluliuma entered Mitanni and pillaged the capital, and then took over North Syria. Aziru, the new king of Amurru, established his control over the Phoenician ports. Akhenaten did not intervene, despite the pleas for help from the Phoenician cities.

He formed an alliance with the king of Assur behind the back of the Babylonian king, who was rather dismayed by the incident.

Finally, Babylon fell into Assyrian control. Egypt then had to share its eastern empire with the two new powers, Hatti and Assyria.

It appears that, towards the end of his life, Akhenaten took on a co-regent, Smenkhkare, thereby breaking the mystic and symbolic union of the perfect couple he formed with Nefertiti. It is even thought that husband and wife no longer lived together. Nefertiti may have withdrawn to her palace, called *Aten's Castle*, located north of Amarna. We know for certain that Smenkhkare was married to the king's oldest daughter Meryt Amun, and was therefore Akhenaten's son-in-law. It seems likely, however, that an even more direct familial link tied him to the sovereign. Several hypotheses have been advanced. Perhaps Smenkhkare was a much younger son of Amenhotep III, or a son of Akhenaten's with a concubine. It's doubtful that he was Ay's son, as has been suggested. He was, in any case, definitely Tutankhamun's brother.

A mummy was found that could be either Smenkhkare's or Akhenaten's. We know Akhenaten was not buried in the tomb that he built at Amarna. It is thus possible that he was secretly transported to a makeshift tomb in the Valley of the Kings, since it was feared that upon his death, his Theban enemies, who were loyal to Amun, would cause trouble.

The events of the end of Akhenaten's reign and the circumstances of his death around 1354 BC remain mysterious. His co-regent Smenhkare succeeded him, but died not long afterwards. This was a turbulent period. The people had not embraced the heretic king's religious reform centered on Aten. Those still faithful to Amun were numerous and influential. Amarna remained a world enclosed upon itself, and the reform seemed doomed to failure. Thebes was hungry for revenge.

Nefertiti and her partisans, led by Ay, wanted to ensure a legitimate succession, perhaps to spare Egypt religious strife, or to avoid retaliation against those faithful to Aten who had persecuted Amun. They proclaimed a young prince of royal blood as pharaoh, the nine-year-old Tutankhaten, husband of little Ankhesenpaaten, daughter of Akhenaten and Nefertiti. Like Smenkhkare, it is speculated that Tutankhaten was a much younger son of Amenhotep III or the son of Akhenaten with a concubine. Neither hypothesis can be confirmed. Tutankhaten was the king who led the country back to tradition.

Tutankhamun's sarcophagus

Three anthropomorphic coffins covered Tutankhamun's mummy. This is the inner one, in solid gold decorated with blue enamel and inlaid with semi-precious stones. It weighs more than 110 kilos (242 avdp) and measures 1.85 meters (6 ft.). The king holds the scepter and flail in his hands, and wears the emblems of Upper and Lower Egypt on his forehead and a false beard.

The restoration

The young king turned away from Aten and changed his name from Tutankhaten to Tutankhamun, "Amun is alive," while his wife Ankhesenpaaten became Ankhesenamun, "she lives for Amun." To mark the revival of the great Theban god, the pharaoh rose to the throne at Karnak.

Two men stood by his side: the principal architect of his ascent to the throne, the "Divine Father" Ay, chief of the chariots, who became his vizier; and a personage whose importance was growing, the General Horemheb, who was an ally of Ay's. When he exited the sanctuary, Tutankhamun was hailed by the joyous crowd, who looked to him to revive Thebes' greatness.

The new sovereign set about to repair the destructions ordered by Akhenaten. He restored the cult of Amun and the other gods, named priests, and erected monuments and statues.

An example is the stele of the "restoration of the temples," for which Tutankhamun undoubtedly drew inspiration from Horemheb (who would later usurp him and erase the young king's name from monuments everywhere).

The great Feast of Opet achieved splendor anew, and art displayed a certain rigour. Statues of the sovereign as Amun were erected everywhere.

The pharaoh was named "he who pleases the gods." A temple was erected for Amun and for the pharaoh's "ka" in the town of Faras, where Huy, viceroy of Nubia, ruled. In the viceroy's tomb, pictures recount Huy's enthronement, the methods he used to collect tributes from the South, and his arrival at Thebes with the flotilla bearing all the produce and the animals that were to be given to the pharaoh.

Another high personage, the General Horemheb, took ever greater ascendancy at the palace, becoming one of the men closest to the pharaoh and amassing military and administrative duties.

Tutankhamun built a funerary temple west of Thebes. Time was too short for him to build a grand tomb, for his mummy reveals that he died at the age of nineteen. He was buried in a small tomb in the Valley of the Kings. When the tomb was discovered in 1922 by Howard Carter, it became instantly famous.

All of Tutankhamun's treasures have survived almost perfectly intact.

Tutankhamun's treasure

Starting in 1917, and with the generous help of Lord Carnavon, a collector passionate about archaeology, Howard Carter led excavations in the Valley of the Kings in the hope of finding Tutankhamun's tomb. By 1922, he was nearly ready to admit defeat. He decided to undertake one last season of excavations in the Valley of the Kings before continuing his research elsewhere.

On November 4, upon arriving at his site, he saw that his team had discovered a step cut into the rock. Full of excitement and doubt, he continued the excavation and discovered a sealed door. Doing his best to keep his exaltation in check, he sent a telegram summoning Lord Carnavon and awaited his arrival. On November 24, the team cleared the steps and discovered Tutankhamun's seals on the door. On the 25th, they removed the door, which opened onto a corridor that also had to be cleared of rubble.

Finally, on November 26 (which Carter later called the happiest day of his life), a second door was penetrated, and, through a candlelit opening, Carter and Lord Carnavon gazed upon "strange animals, statues, and gold – everywhere the glint of gold" that glimmered in the darkened chamber.

Facing page:
Tutankhamun's throne

This wooden throne is covered with gold leaf and inlaid with multicolored stones and glass pieces. On the back of the chair, still in the Amarna style, Ankhesenamun finishes washing her husband, Tutankhamun, with a tender and gentle gesture. Above, the solar disk, Aten, casts rays terminating in hands upon the young royal couple.

Above:
Naos of Tutankhamun's treasury

The alabaster canopic jars containing the king's viscera were placed in this cubic wooden naos stuccoed in gold and topped with a ring of uraeuses (serpents wearing the solar disks as headdresses). Four goddesses keep watch at the cardinal points and protect the deceased as they had once protected Osiris. Here we see Neith and Isis.

Right:
Lid of a canopic jar

The deceased's mummified viscera were locked in four alabaster canopic jars. The four identical lids show the head of the deceased king. Tutankhamun wears the royal headdress topped with the vulture goddess, Nekhbet, and cobra goddess, Wadjet. The whiteness of the alabaster contrasts with the black and red colors of the eyes and mouth.

**Amun
under Tutankhamun's
features**

*The systematic destruction of
Amun's statues during the
Amarna Period probably ex-
plains their rarity. But the
temple at Karnak has provided
us with one of the most beautiful
examples of Amun statuary: the
god, wearing his high crown
with two feathers, appears
under Tutankhamun's features.
His face, though classical,
preserves some characteristics
typical of Amarna.*

First they identified three golden funerary beds
shaped like fantastical animals. Next, they identified
two life-sized statues of the king, in gold and ebony, a
multitude of painted and inlaid boxes, alabaster vases,
flower bouquets, walking sticks, sculpted chairs, a
golden throne, and disassembled golden chariots inlaid
with semi-precious stones. Between the two royal
statues standing guard as sentinels, they saw another
sealed door. Their work had only just begun. First, they
had to clear the first room and take an inventory of its
objects. Under a bed, they found a door leading to a
small and cluttered annex. Its disorderly state, coupled
with traces of hastily sealed breaches in the doors,
indicated that thieves had broken into the tomb and were
forced to make a hasty retreat. Carter undertook a
Herculean task when he set out to describe the numerous
objects consisting of precious furniture, crockery, and
clothing.

The moment finally arrived to open the door at
the back of the antechamber. It led to the funerary
chamber, which contained four chapels that fit one into
another. At the end of the room, a last door opened on
a little chamber that contained the tomb's real treasure.
Carter was awed by a golden tabernacle next to which
stood: the four tutelary goddesses of the deceased; a
statue of Anubis; statues of Tutankhamun astride black
leopards; ivory and wooden boxes inlaid with gold and
a paste of blue glass.

In October 1925, Carter proceeded with the
opening of the four chapels and the sarcophagus. The first
chapel was in gilded wood and inlaid with blue glass.
The second was covered with a veil decorated with gold
daisies. The fourth contained the sarcophagus. Inside,
three coffins fit one inside the other. The first one, in
golden wood, depicted Tutankhamun as Osiris, holding
the scepter and flail. The second, also representing the
king as Osiris, was covered with a thick layer of gold
encrusted with red, blue, and turquoise faience.

The third coffin was in solid gold. It measured
1.85 meters (6 ft.) and weighed 110 kilos (245 avdp.). It
was also anthropomorphic, but the face of the king was
younger. He wore a double collar of red and yellow gold
and blue faience. The coffin contained Tutankhamun's
mummy, blackened by the ointments abundantly spread
on it. The head was covered with a superb golden mask
with the pharaoh's effigy. Roughly one hundred golden
jewels were found on the pharaoh's body.

Horemheb's ascent to power

Little is known about the events following Tutankhamun's death, and this period is steeped in uncertainty. The young pharaoh did not leave an heir, and the succession must have been problematic. The vizier Ay was most likely seen as successor, and may even have been chosen as co-regent by Tutankhamun. During the royal funeral, it was he who performed the ceremony of the opening of the mummy's mouth.

A strange event occurred, unprecedented in Egyptian history, and remains unexplained to this day. The young widow, Ankhesenamun, wrote to Suppiluliuma, the Hittite king, asking for one of his sons in marriage. We do not know at whose prodding the queen undertook this initiative, but we do know that her position at the court, amid intrigues between Ay's partisans and those of Horemheb, was difficult. The Hittite king received this request with surprise and distrust. After much hesitation, he finally sent his son Zannanza to Egypt. But the prince was assassinated on his way, probably at Horemheb's instigation. This triggered war. Suppiluliuma sent an army headed by another of his sons to avenge the murder. The Hittites penetrated Syria, then an Egyptian protectorate. They captured and executed the assassins. General Horemheb went to defend the empire's eastern frontier. It appears that the matter ended there.

Ankhesenamun probably resolved to marry Ay, who was by then fairly old, to legitimise his ascent to the throne. Ay reigned for four years, and displayed tolerance towards the partisans of Aten. He was buried in the Valley of the Monkeys.

Horemheb, "Horus is in Jubilation," succeeded Ay. This general, who had started his career as scribe of the recruits, served under Akhenaten and Tutankhamun.

His name during the Amarna court had been *Paatenemheb*, "Aten is in Jubilation," but he changed it under Tutankhamun. He had become very influential, and had many supporters at the time of Tutankhamun's death. Despite the title he held as general, Horemheb was more interested in legislation than in acts of military brilliance. When Ay died, Horemheb was the most important dignitary in Egypt, more powerful than the vizier or the High Priest. Nothing or nobody opposed his claim to the throne. To reinforce his rights, he married princess Mutnodjmet, Nefertiti's sister.

He must have won over Amun's clergy, for an oracle of the god proclaimed his royalty during a Feast of Opet. Horemheb undertook the country's reorganisation. He wanted to restore order, improve the living conditions of the poverty-stricken masses, and defend the common man against the dishonesty of functionaries who abused the system. He made his plans public in an edict that figures on a stele at Karnak.

To protect the people, prevent thefts, and diminish the power and corruption of the functionaries, he put a series of repressive measures into place, including punishments that were immediately applicable. The new pharaoh usurped Ay's and Tutankhamun's temples and statues and had his

predecessor's names removed. In Thebes, he dismantled the monuments dedicated to Aten and used their talatats and small blocks to build his pylons at Karnak, where he erected the tenth pylon and started the construction of the second, which was later finished by Ramesses II. He built a lane of sphinxes connecting Karnak and Luxor. He was buried in a beautiful hypogeum in the Valley of the Kings.

Texts from the *Book of Porches* first appear here. These are devoted to the regeneration of Re', the solar god. Since Horemheb did not have an heir and felt the need for a warrior king in this difficult conjuncture, he designated his general and vizier Pa-Ramessu, a native of Tanis in the Delta. He would become Ramesses I, founder of the famous Ramesside dynasty.

Horemheb's tomb at Thebes

Before becoming pharaoh, Horemheb was general in the royal army under the commands of Amenhotep IV, Tutankhamun, and Ay. He was thus entitled to build a private tomb for himself, which he did at Sakkara. It was decorated with Amarna reliefs of an extraordinary quality. Once he became pharaoh, he abandoned Sakkara for the Valley of the Kings, where he dug a painted tomb that remained unfinished. The funerary scenes stand out against a blue-grey background.

THE RAMESSES
THE LATE PERIOD

The Ramesside Empire

Horemheb, an astute politician, had designated his chief general and vizier, Pa-Ramessu, to succeed him. Upon the pharaoh's death around 1314 BC, this military man rose to the throne under the name of Ramesses I.

He was an older man whose reign only lasted two years, but he was the founder of an illustrious lineage, the 19th dynasty. His grandson Ramesses II's long reign made the Ramesside era one of military glory, prosperity, and artistic and literary blossoming. Showing great lucidity, Ramesses I immediately named his son Seti, priest of Seth and a military man, to the throne as co-regent.

A warrior pharaoh: Seti I

In 1312 BC, after his father's death, Seti I succeeded him without incident. Continuing the efforts undertaken by Ramesses I, he developed and organised the army and prepared it to fight against the Hatti, whose power, ambition, and claims over Phoenicia posed a grave threat to the Egyptian empire.

Seti divided the infantry, composed of career military men, conscripts drafted in each nome, and mercenaries (mostly Shardana natives of Asia Minor), into three great corps, with Amun, Re', and Ptah as patrons. The chariots were the elite corps, but the Egyptian archers were also renowned. The navy, whose recruits came originally from the Delta, would play an important role in the Ramesside empire.

Seti I first committed himself to the east, to pacify the Shasu Bedouins, from whom he managed to recapture twenty-three fortresses.

In the land of Canaan, he came against a coalition of Amorites and Arameans, backed by the Hittites, and he succeeded in getting the better of them by attacking each enemy corps by surprise. After the Canaan conquest, Seti challenged the Hittites in front of the fortress at Kadesh. King Muwatalli was vanquished by the pharaoh, but the provisory peace ensured by the Egyptian victory did not prevent the Hittite sovereign from fomenting intrigues with the Syrian princes against Egypt. Danger still smouldered.

Seti I also led campaigns in the western frontier, where he checked the threat of a Libyan invasion. In the south, he suppressed a Nubian revolt.

Thanks to this warrior pharaoh, Egypt regained its Asian and African possessions. His predecessors had restored order inside the country.

The country entered a new period of economic development and wealth. A text by Seti I proclaims that his people did not suffer famine during his reign. The sovereign undertook the exploration of the gold mines of the Nubian desert. Water sources, however, were scarce, and the gold diggers could not survive.

Like an authentic sorcerer, Seti crossed the desert and, inspired by the gods, stopped at a precise spot and gave the order for a well to be dug there. Indeed, it contained water. The well was named "Let Re's Divine Justice be Stable."

The pharaoh built a town at that location for those who came to work there, and erected a temple consecrated to Amun, Re', Ptah, Isis, the divine Ennead, and the divinised Seti himself.

Seti I had considerable influence on the building of monuments. He finished the construction of the great hypostyle hall of Amun's temple at Karnak, which his father Ramesses I had begun. He then started its decoration, which Ramesses II later completed.

Pages 100-101:
Ramesses II's chapel
Beyond Thutmose III's buildings, the back of the temple to Amun-Re at Karnak includes a little chapel that was reportedly built by Ramesses II. Of very simple design, it contains a single hall with two colossi of the king, surrounded by eight columns. A socle that used to support an obelisk stands in front of the chapel. The obelisk was removed by Constans II in 357 AD, and is now at Rome's Piazza San Giovanni in Laterano.

Pinodjem I's colossus
The court separating Karnak's first two pylons contains numerous disparate elements without any chronological relationship to each other. This colossus in particular still has not been properly identified. It bears the cartouches of Pinodjem I, a priest of Amun who took on the royal titulary in the 21ˢᵗ dynasty, parallel to the Tanis dynasty. Nevertheless, the Ramesside iconography indicates that the colossus belongs to Ramesses II instead.

This immense hall, intended to serve as a shrine for Amun's sacred barque, was looked upon by the ancients as a marvel. 102 meters (335 ft.) wide and 53 meters (174 ft.) deep, it rises to a maximum height of 24 meters (79 ft.). Its center is formed of two lines of six columns. These twelve main columns are 10 meters (33 ft.) in circumference and 21 meters (69 ft.) in height; their capitals are 15 meters (49 ft.) in circumference and 3 meters (10 ft.) in height. The side aisles contain 122 lower, less massive columns.

This monumental and harmonious complex of 134 papyrus-shaped columns supported a roof, which was pierced between the two ceiling heights by claustra windows, or stone grillwork. These let in the light. The outside of the northern wall is decorated with fine bas-reliefs evoking Seti I's victorious campaigns.

that is reached through seven doors. Ramesses II walled up four of these doors in order to decorate them. At the back of the hall, seven other doors open on a second hypostyle hall, containing three rows of 12 columns, and establishing seven passageways leading to seven chapels dedicated to Amun, Osiris, Iris, Horus, Horakhty, Ptah, and the divinised Seti.

Only the Osiris chapel contains a door leading to other rooms dedicated to the Osirian cult.

All the walls of Seti I's temple are ornamented with incomparably modelled, fine bas-reliefs chiselled in soft limestone.

In the second hypostyle hall, a door flanked by a djed pillar symbolising Osiris opens onto a perpendicular building. The wall of the corridor that connects both wings (called the *Corridor of the Kings*)

Gurnah

Despite a great deal of vandalism, Seti I's funerary temple at Gurnah, on the left bank of the Nile, remains a very beautiful building. It is consecrated to the god Amun of Thebes. The temple's current façade presents a portico with nine columns in the form of papyrus fascicles topped with closed, papyrus-shaped capitals. Under Seti I, these delimited the back of the second court; the rest is almost completely demolished today.

The pharaoh perfected his opus at Karnak by erecting a shrine for the portable barques where the statues of Amun, Mut, and Khonsu were placed during the Feast of Opet.

The most remarkable complex built by Seti I is his "Temple of a Million Years" flanked by a cenotaph, located at Abydos in the site consecrated to Osiris.

The temple, built on a sloping terrain, contains a first hypostyle hall with 24 papyrus-shaped columns

bears the famous *Royal List of Abydos*, a series of seventy-six pharaohs' cartouches from Narmer to Seti I.

Seti I's cenotaph leans against the funerary temple. It was inaccurately named the Osireion, because when first cleared, it was thought that Osiris' tomb had been discovered. It is built as a hypogeum in a rocky hillock. The walls of the long descending corridor are covered with excerpts from the *Book of Gates* and the

Book of Caverns. The walls of a great transversal hall are decorated with scenes and quotes from the *Book of the Dead*. The cenotaph itself is a large hall supported by five pink-granite pillars that originally contained a mound emerging from a moat, symbol of the primordial mound. In a last room, named Sarcophagus Hall, the ceiling is ornamented with a superb representation of the queen of the sky, Nut.

Nevertheless, Seti I built his true tomb in the Valley of the Kings. It is a vast hypogeum, decorated with paintings depicting scenes from funerary books. His mummy was not there; it was found in the hiding place at Deir el-Bahari.

Among his sons, the pharaoh himself chose prince Ramesses, son of Tuy, as his successor. From a very young age, the king initiated him in the art of war. He took the prince on campaigns as early as the age of ten, and taught him how to lead an army to victory.

The young heir was initiated just as early in the art of love; when he was ten, he was given a harem by his father.

Very quickly, Seti I named his son to the throne as co-regent, perhaps from the sixth year of his reign, when Ramesses was sixteen years old. The sovereign conferred the full title to the future Ramesses II from the co-regency onwards.

Ramesses II the Great

At Seti I's death, around 1296 BC, Ramesses II (in Egyptian, "Ra-mes-su," "It is Re' who gave birth to him") took succession immediately and organised a grand funeral for his father. The new pharaoh was just twenty-five, but already had leadership experience. His reign, one of the longest and most glorious of Egyptian history, lasted sixty-seven years. The Empire then achieved its apogee, and its sovereign entered posterity under the name of Ramesses the Great.

From the beginning of his reign, Ramesses II, a warrior king, prepared for a great military campaign. The situation in Syria was disquieting. The Hittite danger became clearer. King Muwatalli formed alliances with the Syrian princes and spread his influence, little by little, over the Egyptian protectorates in Asia.

Ramesses II and his troops departed on the Asian route towards Kadesh and the Amurru, key points where Egyptian hegemony in the Orient played out. He crossed Canaan and Phoenicia without obstacles, managed to reaffirm his ascendancy over the kingdom of Amurru, and returned to Egypt.

Mutawalli then called upon his vassals and allies in Asia Minor and North Syria, and became the head of a substantial coalition of twenty peoples, including the Dardanians, the Lyceans, the Mysians, the land of Naharina, Phoenician cities such as Ugarit, and the Syrian citadels of Karkemish, Harran, Alep, and Kadesh.

Ramesses II took the eastern route again, followed by his entire infantry, comprised now of four army corps, those of Amun, Re', and Ptah, to which the pharaoh added a fourth corps under the protection of Seth, god of Tanis, the Ramesside city of origin. Not far from Kadesh, the Egyptians seized two Bedouins and interrogated them. They claimed to be deserters from the Hittite army wanting to join the Egyptian ranks, and affirmed that Muwatalli and his allies were to be found near Alep, 200 kilometers (124 miles) from Kadesh.

The pharaoh, at the head of Amun's army, advanced towards Kadesh and settled his encampment at the banks of the Oronte, where he thought he would await the rest of his troops. It was then that Egyptian scouts brought over two Hittite soldiers that they had captured.

Seti I at Gurnah

The bas-reliefs in the temple at Gurnah, like those at Karnak and Abydos, reveal Seti I's particularly refined taste. The pharaoh, wearing royal attributes, addresses the Theban Triad in an attitude of veneration and with extremely delicate gestures. Unlike his successor Ramesses II, Seti I uses bas-relief sculpture.

They were tortured and confessed Muwatalli's ruse: the members of the coalition were regrouped at Kadesh and were three kilometers (1.8 miles) from the Egyptian camp.

Unfortunately, Ramesses' forces were dispersed. The army of Re' had yet to join that of Amun, led by the pharaoh.

The Ptah and Seth divisions were still far away. Ramesses sent the vizier over to the army of Re' to hurry its march, but it suffered a surprise attack by the Hittites and was wrecked. The situation seemed desperate. The enemy launched an attack on the Amun division. When they saw the Hittite chariots advancing upon them, the pharaoh's soldiers knew they were outnumbered and fled in fear.

At this point in the story, history yields to myth.

Ramesses, like the warrior god Mentu, drove his chariots into the enemy ranks. He quickly found himself surrounded by 2500 Hittite chariots, accompanied only by his terrified but faithful charioteer, Menna.

The hero-king then addressed a fervent prayer to Amun. The god answered his call and Ramesses, animated by the divine force, decimated the Hittite chariotry. He single-handedly paralysed the enemy. The night of the massacre, the Egyptian deserters returned. The day after, Ramesses and his army attacked. It was victory: Muwatalli abandoned the combat and made Ramesses a peace proposal. This celebrated battle of Kadesh would turn out to be but a half-victory, however; the city had not fallen, and peace was provisional.

The battle of Kadesh

In the fifth year of his reign, Ramesses II won a blody victory ofer the Hittites. To immortalise his success, he hat mumerous representations of this battle made on monuments erected to this means. Here, the second pylon of the Ramesseum shows scenes of the battle as well as citing the Poem of the Pentour, writen for the occasion.

Soon after, the king of Hatti launched new hostilities, triggering revolts in the Land of Canaan and forcing the pharaoh to set out for another Asian campaign. Then Muwatalli died, and Ramesses took advantage of the interlude created by the Hittite succession quarrels to conquer eight towns. Afterwards, he led a pacification campaign in the Sudan.

But then the Assyrian king Salmanasar I invaded Mitanni. Faced with the danger that this new power represented, Egypt and Hatt (led by its new king, Hattusil III) decided to form an alliance. They drew up a peace treaty, and its text is the oldest peace treaty ever found. It was written in the twenty-first year of Ramesses II's reign, that is, in 1275 BC. The Hittite copy was placed at Heliopolis, at the feet of the god Re'.

It was translated into Egyptian and engraved on the walls of several temples, including Karnak and Abu Simbel. The Egyptian text was placed at the feet of the god Teshup and copied on clay tablets that were placed in the Hittite archives.

This treaty inaugurated an era of economic exchanges and prosperity for the two signatory powers. The alliance was renewed twelve years later, through Ramesses' marriage to a Hittite princess. She was received by the Egyptian dignitaries and taken to Pi-Ramesses, where the pharaoh was waiting for her. Henceforth she was named Maathorneferure.

This marriage and the young woman's long voyage must have tickled minds; it inspired various legends, including the tale of the *Princess of Bakhtan*. It tells the story of the marriage of a pharaoh to a foreign princess whose youngest sister is suffering from an incurable disease. The princess sends for a magician from Thebes. The scholar answers that only an Egyptian god can save her, and sends her a statue of Khonsu. As soon as the statue arrives, the princess' sister is cured.

Ramesses' conquests, like those of Thutmose in earlier times, brought Egypt rich tributes from all over, as well as Mediterranean and Oriental merchants. Abundance became the country's rule.

Thanks to the pharaoh, Thebes was one of the richest, most prosperous cities. Commerce flourished, and Ramesses understood the need for a great port to receive the substantial Mediterranean traffic. Taking up Thutmose III's idea, he set up a seaport facing the island

of Pharos, northwest of the Delta, where the Greek and Phoenician boats always stopped, on the site that would later become Alexandria.

The sovereign also developed the Memphis port and industries, which went through renewed prosperity. It was in Memphis, which from the onset was dedicated to the god Ptah, *Lord of the Jubilees*, that Ramesses II and his son Khaemwaset, High Priest of Ptah, built an imposing Jubilee Palace. This is where Ramesses' first jubilee, or Sed festival, took place.

This ceremony was meant to renew the pharaoh's power. It started with a procession. Then, in the presence of the gods, princes, high dignitaries, and ambassadors from all countries in the empire, the king performed a ritual meant to symbolise his taking possession of the earth. Dressed with a sheathing cloth, his skin painted green like Osiris, he mimed his own rebirth, thus completing the cycle of life and death, like vegetation and like the soul in the hereafter. Finally, the crowning ceremony was re-enacted. In this way, the king regained the plenitude of his force and his mastery of the world. Ramesses II celebrated at least thirteen jubilees.

The city of Thebes continued to flourish. The Greek and Phoenician boats that rode the Nile delivered merchandise and new ideas; foreign merchants even settled there for trade. As city of Amun, it maintained its religious supremacy, but it lost its role of capital of the empire.

For his capital, Ramesses II chose a new city, which he built on the site of Avaris, in the outer eastern limits of the Delta, not far from Tanis. He named it Pi-Ramesses, *Ramesses' House.*

The capital was built around an ancient summer palace erected by Ramesses I, which Seti I had turned into his residence, and which Ramesses II enlarged. It contained a prestigious complex of temples and official buildings, a residential quarter with luxurious villas surrounded by gardens, a port, and popular quarters.

The court lived in luxury at Pi-Ramesses. The king owned a harem, but only the wives and the

The Ramesseum

Ramesses II's funerary temple, now named Ramesseum, remains one of the most complete buildings of the Theban necropolis because it still contains annexed structures in mud brick. One enters through a powerful pylon that gives access to a court, bordered with porticoes, in which lay the debris of an immense colossus of Ramesses that must have measured more than 17 meters (56 ft.) in height. Then follow a second pylon, a court in ruins, a large hypostyle hall, and, finally, the sanctuary.

Pages 108-109:
Ramesses II's court at Luxor

True to his fame as a great builder, Ramesses II added a court to the temple at Luxor even more spacious than Amenhotep III's, measuring 50 meters (164 ft.) wide and 57 meters (187 ft.) long. Originally bordered by porticoes on all four sides and preceded by two obelisks, six colossal statues, and one pylon, the Ramesside court has suffered due to the establishment of the Muslim saint Abu el-Haggag's mosque.

Facing page:
Sennedjem's tomb

Sennedjem's tomb, "servant in the Place of Truth," dates from the 20th dynasty and is found in the necropolis of Deir el-Medineh, a town built by the artisans of the Valley of the Kings. What is surprising about this tomb is its multicolored vividness, which survived almost intact to this day. The burial vault is entirely covered with religious scenes pertaining to the deceased's voyage in the hereafter. The baboon, often assimilated to the god Thot, figures here as a lunar god and a god of wisdom, functions that very quickly establish a connection with the funerary cult of Osiris.

The Luxor obelisk

Of the two obelisks at Luxor, only the eastern one is still on site. The western one is now on the Place de la Concorde in Paris. Mehmet Ali gave it to France in 1831. Erected by Ramesses II, the obelisks measure between 21 and 25 (69 and 82 ft.) meters high. The engraved scenes represent an immense homage to the god Re', followed by the king's protocol and a text about his constructions, his victories, and his reign.

important concubines lived in the capital. The greater part of the harem was found in the Fayum, where the pharaoh entertained himself also by hunting and fishing. Ramesses had five Great Royal Wives: Nefertari, his favorite; Istonfret, mother of his successor Merenptah; Hetmire, his own sister; Maathorneferure, the Hittite princess; and Bent-Anat, his own daughter.

Nefertari, his main wife, always appeared at his side in official ceremonies. It seems that she had a certain political influence. She was a brilliant sovereign, considered a veritable incarnation of Isis and Hathor, and was profoundly loved. The king associated her to his divine glory and united the two of them for all eternity by dedicating her a little temple next to the great temple that he built at Abu Simbel. He built her a beautiful tomb in the Valley of the Queens, where gracious paintings with lively colors outline the fine, elegant silhouette of the pretty Nefertari.

The many women of his harem gave Ramesses II abundant descendants: fifty sons and fifty-three daughters. This number is the minimum, as it includes only the names of royal children cited on the lists engraved on the temples. With Nefertari, the pharaoh had four sons, including Mery-Atum, High Priest of Re', and two daughters.

The second wife, Istonfret, was the mother of Bent-Anat (who Ramesses later married) and three sons, two of whom played a great role. Khaemwaset was favored by his father, who had hoped to make him his successor. He was High Priest of Ptah at Memphis and guardian of the necropolis of the Apis bulls. The prince restored the texts of the pyramids of kings from the fifth and sixth dynasties, notably those of Unas, Userkaf, Sahure, and Niuserre (fifth dynasty), as well as King Djoser's (third dynasty). Khaemwaset was a scholar. He died before his father and entered legend as a savant and magician.

It was Merenptah, Istonfret's second son, who Ramesses then chose as heir. He was general-in-chief of the army and royal scribe. He was equally charged with the bulls' necropolis. He had great influence on the pharaoh. During the last twelve years of reign, when Ramesses II was quite aged, it was Merenptah who held the reins of power.

The great sovereign knew to surround himself with high functionaries who proclaimed, on their rich tombs in the Theban necropolis, their loyalty and zeal in accomplishing their functions. The kingdom's two most powerful dignitaries were the viziers. Since Thutmose III, a vizier governed Lower Egypt and another governed Upper Egypt. Three prestigious viziers marked Ramesses II's reign. Paser, son of the High Priest of Amun Nebneteru, was already in office under Seti I, and exercised his administrative, judiciary, financial, and economic high functions with loyalty and fairness until about the twentieth year of reign.

Paser's family was very influential. Paser himself also held the post of mayor of Thebes. His father was High Priest of Amun, and his son, Amenemipet, was viceroy of Kush. Khay, one of the pharaoh's sons, succeeded Paser. Finally, Rehotep accumulated the offices of vizier and High Priest of Maat, Re', and Ptah.

Ramesses II's reign was a period of intense cultural activity in the religious domain and in literary and architectural creation.

Ever since the Old Kingdom, a tendency towards syncretism was one of the major elements of Egyptian religion. The Ramesside theologians developed a synthesis associating Amun, Re', and Ptah. This trinity expressed the divine being. Re', who represented the shining face of the god, was himself

The Sema Tawy

The Sema Tawy, or "reunion of the two lands," harks back to the first dynasty when Narmer united Upper and Lower Egypt in a single kingdom. Two Hapi gods, personifications of the Nile floods, tie the two heraldic plants with the help of a rope: the South's lotus and the North's papyrus. The plants themselves are tied around the hieroglyphic sign "Sema," meaning "to unite." Sometimes the Hapi gods are replaced by Horus and Seth.

a syncretism of: Re' (the solar globe), Horakhty (the celestial falcon, Horus of the Horizon), Khepri (the rising sun), and Atum (the setting sun). Moreover, the union of Re' and Osiris symbolised the complementary sides of life and death. Just as Re' dies in the west, undertakes a nocturnal voyage to Osiris' subterranean kingdom, and is reborn in the east, so the "Lord of the Dead" dies and is resuscitated again.

Ramesses II encouraged the opening of Egyptian religion to foreign gods.

The god of the tempest, Baal, was associated with Seth. The pharaoh founded a cult of Baal-Seth at Pi-Ramesses. The warrior gods were particularly honored: Resheph, who was also fused with Seth, and above all the goddess Astarte or Anat. A falcon god, Hurun, was assimilated to Horakhty.

The kingdom's most powerful religious dignitary then was the High Priest of Amun.

Under Ramesses II, the following succeeded in this office: Nebwenef, Unennefer, the vizier Paser, and finally Paser's son Bekenkhons, the most eminent of them all. This proud and wise man, faithful to his god and his king, is associated with the construction of the temple Ramesses II built at Luxor.

In front of the temple's pylon, he erected the obelisk that is now found at the Place de la Concorde in Paris.

At first, the sovereign assigned the great Re' priesthood to military men whom he wished to honor: Bak, then Amenemipet. It then fell to Mery-Atum, Ramesses II's son, and to vizier Rehotep.

The most eminent High Priests of Ptah were Khaemwaset (the pharaoh's son) and Rehotep.

The high priest, or "first servant of the god," administrated the temple's material wealth and ran a substantial clergy, which comprised: the servants of the god; high-ranking priests allowed to contemplate the divinity; lector-priests; the famous savant-magicians who knew all the rites; astronomer-priests; and, lastly, pure priests charged with washing the god. The pontiff also directed a whole world of laymen associated with the life of the temple: administrators, scribes, musicians, and singers.

The Egyptian temple was a privileged space where the divine manifested itself, a sort of point of contact between the earthly and the spiritual. It was the "house of the god," conceived as a fortress, closed to the faithful masses.

The priests who oversaw the divinity had to help him accomplish his main task: to maintain the divine order present at creation. For that they had to protect the god from all soiling, spiritual or material; nourish him; and worship him daily according to immutable rites.

Each morning at dawn, the priests went in procession to the sacred lake to purify themselves. Then they entered the temple, lit the door of the sanctuary, and continued to the naos, which housed the statue inhabited by the god's soul, all while reciting prayers and burning incense. Representing the pharaoh, the high priest embraced the statue and presented it with the offering of a statuette of Maat, symbol of the world's balance. Awoken by these rites, the god received an offering of nourishment.

Then he was washed, clothed, perfumed, and covered with jewels. After removing every trace of human presence, the priests finally closed the sanctuary again, taking with them the foods from which the god had drawn his energy and distributing them afterwards. Prayers and the burning of incense took place at noon and in the evening.

As the years passed, literature blossomed and the Ramesside era witnessed the flourishing of love poetry as well as mythological legends, moral tales, and, of course, hymns to the gods and the pharaoh.

A mischievous legend features Isis, the magician, and the powerful Re'. At the time when the gods dwelled upon the earth, Isis wished to know Re's secret name, which was tantamount with possessing supreme knowledge and power over the great god. She imagined a subterfuge and created a serpent that she placed on Re's route. The god, bitten by the serpent, was stricken with terrible pains and called his children for help. Isis then told him that she could heal him if he revealed his name to her. Re' gave in, and the magician destroyed the evil that she herself had created.

Ramesses II was a great builder. He had an abundant workforce at his disposal, consisting of free men – Egyptians and foreigners – and enslaved war prisoners. It was probably under his reign that the Exodus took place.

Many Hebrew workers had settled in Egypt as free men, and it is not known if they decided to depart on their own initiative or whether they were expelled from the kingdom by the pharaoh.

The sovereign first set out to beautify Luxor and Karnak. He depicted scenes from his military victories on the south wall of Ramesses I's and Seti I's great hypostyle hall at Karnak. He erected two colossi with his effigy at the entrance of the second pylon.

He built a temple extending Amenhotep III's edifice at Luxor, and erected two pink-granite obelisks in front of its pylon. At the entrance he placed four colossi depicting himself sitting next to Nefertari on his throne, and two standing ones of himself alone.

The grandest monumental complex that Ramesses II erected, with the help of his royal steward Yuny, is undoubtedly the one at Abu Simbel, consisting of two rock temples cut into the Nubian cliff.

The largest, southern one is consecrated to Amun-Re and to the pharaoh himself. The east-facing façade rises to a height of 31 meters (102 ft). Four 20-meter- (66 ft.-) high colossi flank the entrance gate. They depict the king sitting on his throne next to his family, in a smaller dimension. Above the gate, a niche houses a falcon-headed statue of Re'-Horakhty wearing the solar disk. On the cornice there is a frieze of twenty-two baboons greeting the rising sun.

The temple, cut into the rock to a depth of up to 55 meters (180 ft.), contains two large pillared halls, various annexed chambers, and a sanctuary where four statues of Ptah, Amun, Ramesses II, and Re'-Horakhty are sculpted in the rock. The first pillared hall is decorated with war scenes, most of them in remembrance of the battle of Kadesh. The second is ornamented with religious scenes where the king and queen find their place amongst the gods.

The hypostyle hall at Karnak

The great hypostyle hall at Karnak offers such a spectacle to the eyes that, since Antiquity, travellers have stood in wonderment in front of this "forest of columns": 122 columns with closed capitals surround the 12 colossal columns of the central aisle.

A smaller one, on the north, is dedicated to the goddess Hathor and to Nefertari. The façade, also facing east, is dug with niches housing six colossal standing statues that are 10 meters (33 ft.) high. Two of them represent the queen as Hathor, flanked on each side by statues of the king. A great hall with Hathoric pillars (bearing the goddess' head with cow ears and a beautiful head of curly hair) is covered with representations of the royal couple in the company of divinities.

At the time of the development of Lake Nasser, when the Nile waters were held back by the construction of an immense dam, the two temples at Abu Simbel were threatened with destruction on account of the rising waters. In 1960, UNESCO organised an international rescue plan. The mountain was dug all around the monuments to clear them. The monuments were cut in enormous blocks, whose total weight reached 15000 tons.

The whole lot was rebuilt 180 meters (590 ft) further away, over the rocky plateau that was 64 meters (210 ft) higher, on a concrete cupola covered with stones from the quarry to reproduce the rocky setting.

viewers are still enthralled by the diversity of its materials even today: the grey granite of a statue group that includes Amun, Seti I, and Ramesses II; the white limestone of two chapels dedicated to Isis and Horus; the black granite of the gates' frames; the sandstone of the pillars in the hypostyle halls; and the pure alabaster and yellow quartzite of the Osirian sanctuary with a pink-granite ceiling.

Here, the refinement of the materials combines with the elegance of the bas-reliefs depicting war or rustic themes. Its delicate style is closer to the works created under Seti I than to the majestic art that was in fashion under Ramesses II.

The great pharaoh constructed his "Temple of a Million Years," the Ramesseum, on Thebes' left bank. This gigantic building contained: the funerary temple itself, composed of two pylons; two peristyle courts; a large hypostyle hall with 48 columns, followed by three smaller halls and the sanctuary; annexed brick buildings serving as stores and homes for the personnel; a school for scribes and artists; a small temple dedicated to Seti; and finally a royal palace.

Abu Simbel

Considered one of the great technical feats of Egyptian architecture, the two speos temples built by Ramesses II at Abu Simbel, south of the first cataract, have an astonishingly colossal yet harmonious appearance. The first was dedicated to Egypt's two principal gods, Amun-Re' from Thebes and Re'-Horakhty of Heliopolos. The second, more modest, celebrated the goddess Hathor and the divinised Queen Nefertari.

Ramesses II built three other rock temples in Nubia that were also transferred – those of Derr, consecrated to Amun-Re'; Wadi es-Sebua, dedicated to Amun-Re' and Re'-Horakhty, and having a dromos; and Bet el-Wali. The sovereign also restored the building of Amada, built by Thutmose III, Amenhotep II, and Thutmose IV in honor of Amun and Re'-Horakhty. The temple was moved in one piece with the help of a concrete socle and rails.

Ramesses restored and completed his father Seti I's monument at Abydos, building a pylon and two courts in front of the temple. He also erected his own temple, which is in terrible condition now. Nevertheless,

Even in its deteriorated state of today, the complex is charming, graceful and elegant.

Ramesses II died around 1229 BC, aged 92, after reigning for sixty-seven years. He was buried in his vast hypogeum of the Valley of the Kings, built by the architect Suti, who was also first charioteer and chief of the royal treasure.

His mummy, found in the hiding place at Deir el-Bahari, was flown to Paris in 1976 with great precaution, and was submitted to the care of modern science. Once restored, it was returned to Egypt. It was received by dignitaries, and a military detachment paid homage to the great sovereign's mortal remains.

Preserving the Empire

Merenptah, the son whom Ramesses II had chosen as heir, was crowned in 1229 BC. He was an older man who had held power during the last twelve years of his father's reign. His own reign lasted about ten years.

When Merenptah ascended to the throne, a new danger threatened Egypt in the form of "The peoples of the Sea." This was the name the Egyptians gave to the Achaeans and the peoples of Asia Minor (the Mycenaeans, Lydians, Carians, and Lycians) who had been pushed by the Dorian invasions towards Phoenicia, Canaan, and Libya, and beyond them into Egypt. Most of them first invaded Libya, or the land of Tjehenu; among them were the Libu, who gave their name to the country. From Libya, they threatened to penetrate Egypt.

After having harshly repressed an uprising in the land of Kush, Merenptah concentrated his forces on the Libyan frontier. The invaders had chosen a leader, Merey, and under his command they managed to advance as far as the Delta. It was there, at Perire, that the battle took place. Vanquished and dethroned, the Libyan chief fled when faced with the magnitude of the Egyptian troops. The pharaoh's victorious army crossed the Delta, loaded with an immense booty of captives, animals, gold, and weapons. Merenptah erected a victory column at Heliopolis and a stele celebrating the return of peace at Karnak.

The sovereign had managed to hold on to the Ramesside empire. But the high clergy, whose riches and power had become ever greater under Ramesses II, was threatening royal authority. Great priestly families accumulated the highest religious and administrative offices and eroded the pharaoh's power little by little.

Merenptah named his son, Seti-Merenptah, born of a Great Royal Wife, co-regent to the throne. Despite this, when he died around 1218 BC, something must have occurred that we are unaware of, because it was an usurper, Amenmesses and not the legitimate heir who took the throne. This Amenmesses was most likely a son of the king and a concubine, and he reigned for a few years until Seti-Merenptah re-captured power.

Seti-Merenptah was crowned around 1213 BC under the name of Seti II.

Seti II

We know little about pharaoh Seti II, who reigned at the end of the 19th dynasty, from around 1200 BC, for probably fewer than ten years. The cartouches engraved on the two arms of this very beautiful sandstone statue allow us to read the king's fourth name, Usirkheperure, accompanied by the determinative ritual, Mery-Amun ("Amun's beloved").

Seti II tried to check the deterioration of royal power by placing reliable men in the administration's key posts. But the power of the high priests and their families continued to grow, tearing the central authority.

The sovereign had a Great Royal Wife named Tausret, with whom he apparently did not have a son. At his death, around 1206 BC, the country's situation was anarchic, and a young boy, Ramesses Siptah, perhaps the son of Seti II and a concubine, rose to the throne. After two years' reign he changed his title to Merenptah Siptah.

Queen Tausret took the role of a sort of regent. With the help of her chancellor, Bay, who was most likely a Syrian native, she seized control. It is possible that the young king was manipulated by the two accomplices.

The queen even married Siptah and, upon his death, Tausret took the royal title and reigned as pharaoh for a few turbulent years marked by internal troubles. When she died, the country was on the verge of anarchy and civil war. A Syrian, Irsu, even managed to snatch power.

Finally, a certain Setnakht ("Seth is powerful"), undoubtedly a military man, succeeded in taking control of the kingdom. In two years of reign, he put an end to civil war and re-established order in Egypt. He was the founder of a new dynasty, the 20th. His legitimate son and successor, Ramesses III, would be Egypt's last great warrior pharaoh.

Ramesses III, Egypt's saviour

Ramesses III was crowned around 1198 BC. He was celebrated by his joyous subjects, who were happy to see the country reunited. Peace may have returned to the country's interior, but the situation at the frontiers was disquieting. The danger from the Peoples of the Sea became sharper, threatening Egypt to the west and to the north.

The world of Antiquity was going through profound changes. The Indo-European peoples disturbed the Middle East's balance. By their gigantic migration, they devastated everything in their path as they searched for new countries in which to settle. To the west, the Libu immigrants from Asia Minor who had established in Libya allied themselves with the

considered himself an invincible military chief. He prepared to confront the Peoples of the Sea, whose presence at Egypt's frontiers became ever more pressing. He organised his infantry and chariotry, and created a "wall" of war boats at the mouth of the Nile.

The pharaoh fought against the Peoples of the Sea for eleven years at the frontiers – eleven years of victorious battles, punctuated by the loot-bearing army's triumphant homecomings and by preparations for new attacks. Ramesses III led two wars on the western front against Libyan troops, and a gigantic battle in the north, over land and sea, against the coalition of the Peoples of the Sea. The pharaoh's victory was complete, and the kingdom was safe. In the twelfth year of his reign, the pharaoh left for a campaign in Asia, in an attempt to safeguard his Syrian

ancient Libyan tribes (the Timhiu, the Tjehenu, and the Berber Meshwesh) to try to invade prosperous Egypt. To the north, the Indo-European populations invaded Asia and devastated Hatti, Naharina, Amarru, Phoe-nicia, and Canaan, where they formed a vast coalition to attack Egypt by land and sea.

Ramesses III thought of himself as heir and spiritual son of the great Ramesses II. He was imbued with his role as the country's defender, and he

possessions. By the beginning of the 12th century BC, the Eastern World had been turned upside down.

The powerful Hittite Empire and the Phoenician civilisation did not exist anymore. Canaan fell into the hands of the Philistines, who gave it the name of Palestine. Egypt alone had been able to withstand the onslaught of the Peoples of the Sea. Once peace was re-established, the kingdom recovered its former prosperity.

Ramesses VI's tomb

The sarcophagus hall of Ramesses VI's tomb in the Valley of the Kings. The astronomical ceiling, divided into two panels by two depictions of the goddess Nut, shows a decadent yet very original art. Astronomical divinities, painted yellow, take part in the navigation of the solar barques across the celestial Nile.

Commerce flourished anew and the pharaoh even organised an expedition to Punt.

Ramesses III made sumptuous gifts to temples throughout the country. To this end, he ordered a census of all the Egyptian temples and divinities. The priestly families again had wealth and power. The High Priest of Amun, Bekenkhons, gained considerable military functions attached to his religious office.

At Karnak, Ramesses built a vast yellow sandstone shrine for the barques of the Theban Triad, and two temples consecrated to the goddess Mut and the god Khonsu. Nevertheless, the sovereign's most important monument is his "Temple of a Million Years" at Medinet Habu, on Thebes' left bank. The pylons bear two hymns celebrating the pharaoh's glory and a victorious Egypt. On the inside walls are depicted episodes of the feast of Min, the god of procreation who presides over fecundity and fertility. The king who had managed to protect the country from enemy attacks saw his reign end amid intrigue and conspiracy.

A broad plot arose involving Queen Tiy and her son Pentaur, with the objective of suppressing the king and installing Pentaur on the throne. Among the schemers were harem high functionaries, a superintendent, a royal treasurer, scribes, overseers, and even the harem's women participated. They performed bewitchment rites on wax figurines. These were meant to make the gate guardians fall asleep so that those within the palace could let in outside conspirators, with whom messages had been exchanged.

The plot was substantial indeed; a commander of the Nubian archers and a general were involved, and they roused the troops and fomented trouble in the country in preparation of a coup d'état. But someone must have betrayed the guilty parties, for they were arrested, tried, and condemned to death.

Ramesses III died not long afterwards. He had several sons with the Great Royal Wife Isis. Three of them would reign, under the names of Ramesses IV, Ramesses VI, and Ramses VIII.

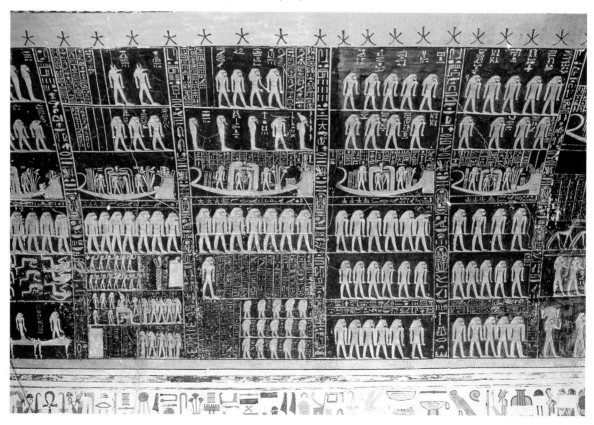

The Late Period
Decadence

Ancient Egypt's glorious history ends with Ramesses III. The country entered a long twilight. The great Ramesses' successors allowed the country's internal situation to deteriorate little by little, thereby exposing the kingdom to foreign ambitions.

Ramesses IV was crowned in 1166 BC. He managed to preserve his father's opus and to maintain a certain prosperity. After his death, six years later, the 20th dynasty entered a dark period that would lead to an inglorious end.

Under the last Ramesses, the clergy became ever more powerful and venal, and the royal power ever weaker. People lived in poverty.

Under the reigns of Ramesses VII and his successors, disastrous harvests led to years of famine. Anarchy and corruption were widespread: "thefts and depredations over the sacred domains, functionaries' venality, usurpation of sacerdotal offices (…) and local feud-settling. (…) As to the countless workers and artists (…) they threw themselves upon the royal tombs of the western shore of Thebes to pillage them, trying to escape the terrible years of poverty and famine through sacrilege." (Serge Saumeron).

This started happening under Ramesses IX, during whose reign exorbitant privileges were accorded to the High Priest of Amun.

Under Ramesses IX, Libyans, who had gradually settled in Egypt, became very influential. They made a failed attempt to take over power. And yet the pharaoh allowed his vizier Herihor, who was also High Priest of Amun, generalissimo and viceroy of Nubia, to govern in his place.

The last of the Ramesses apparently ended up abdicating around 1085. The New Kingdom was over, and an era of slow decadence called the Late Period took its place, during which Egypt went through division and foreign domination, but also experienced some brilliant times.

In 1085, Herihor gave himself the title of "son of Amun." His power extended over Upper Egypt only. He founded the 21st Theban dynasty, a theocratic dynasty of High Priests of Amun such as Pinodjem I and Pinodjem II.

Denderah

The walls between the columns at Denderah show just how far the Roman colonisers had adopted Egyptian civilisation in its smallest details. At right, the emperor, wearing the royal crown, offers a rising sun to Hathor, followed by Horus.

The temple of Philae

The oldest buildings of the sanctuary of Isis at Philae date from the 30th dynasty and King Nectanebo I, but most of the elements date from the Ptolemaic dynasty. Construction continued even under the Roman emperors – witness Trajan's kiosk. In the mid 6th century AD, Justinian closed the temple of Philae, thus ending the cult of Isis in Egypt.

Just as in the darkest periods of its history, the kingdom was divided. Lower Egypt's vizier, Smendes, reigned at Tanis, in the Delta. He was the founder of the 21st Tanite dynasty, whose kings included Psusennes I, Amenophthis, Saamun, and Psusennes II. Under the 21st dynasty, the pillaging of the tombs in the Valley of the Kings continued at a fast pace, and the priests were forced to transfer the royal mummies to hiding places at Deir el-Bahari. The monuments of Pi-Ramesses were destroyed to build the new Tanis.

In 945 BC, a sovereign of Libyan origin, Sheshonq I, took power in Tanis and managed to reunite Egypt by imposing his authority over the Theban high priests. He inaugurated the 22nd dynasty, which included pharaohs named Sheshonq, Osorkon, and Takelot, under whom Lower Egypt had a period of prosperity and economic and commercial growth.

During those times, the little Hebrew kingdom founded by King David, who had liberated the country from the Philistines, flourished thanks to the monopoly that King Salomon had established over the commercial route linking the Mediterranean with Arabia.

Salomon had been very powerful, but after his death Sheshonq I attacked and took Jerusalem in 925 BC. The Egyptian army pillaged the Temple's treasures and the royal palace, returning to Tanis with sumptuous loot. The capital and the whole Delta then lived in opulence, while Upper Egypt fell prey to feudalization and opposition to progress.

Under Sheshong III, the Delta was partitioned. Egypt itself was once again divided and fell into anarchy. Its eventual reunification was due to an Ethiopian (or, rather, Kushite) prince, Piankhi. The Ethiopian dynasty tried to push back the Assyrian assault that threatened the Delta. But Assurbanipal succeeded in penetrating Egypt and taking Thebes in 667 BC.

To be accepted by his Egyptian subjects, Alexander proclaimed himself "son of Amun" by the oracle at Siwa and was crowned following the pharaonic ritual. He created the city of Alexandria, a new capital where his successors, the Ptolemys, also reigned.

The Greek kings revived tradition by building sumptuous temples in the classical style, such as Edfu, Denderah, Kom Ombo, Esna, and Philae, all worthy of figuring among the masterpieces of Egyptian architecture. In cosmopolitan Alexandria, however, Greek culture flourished and transformed itself in the fecund brew of peoples and ideas. A new civilisation was born, neither Hellenic nor Egyptian. It would continue to blossom well after the fall of Ptolemaic Egypt in 30 BC, under the celebrated Queen Cleopatra, who was vanquished by Rome.

The temple at Esna

The interior of the hypostyle hall at Esna shows some beautiful examples of columns with composite capitals.

The temple at Edfu

The temple to Horus at Edfu remains one of the most renowned in all of Egypt thanks to the clarity of its layout. In the back, the sanctuary houses a superb naos in black granite, more than four meters high. The colossal statue of the god Horus, represented as a falcon wearing the double crown of Egypt, has been the highlight of this temple famous since Antiquity.

In 664 BC, Psamtek I took power and expelled Ethiopians and Assyrians. His dynasty, the 26th, was called the "Saite Renaissance." The newly reorganized state became strong once again.

Nevertheless, it could not resist the formidable Persian army that assailed it; in 525 BC the Persian Cambyses rose to the Egyptian throne. His son, Darius I, succeeded him. The Egyptians rebelled and succeeded in chasing the Persians out of their country for some time. But the 30th dynasty was the last one. Under pharaoh Nectanebo II, the Persian Ataxerxes III invaded Egypt. It was the end of independence.

In 332 BC, Alexander the Great freed the country from the Persian yoke, only to impose upon it the Greek dynasties.

GLOSSARY

AMULETS: Small symbolic objects worn by the living or by the dead to protect them.

THE ANKH: A looped cross symbolising eternal life.

BA: The spiritual entity of a human being which corresponds more or less to our notion of the "soul." The Ba is represented as a bird with a human head; it leaves the body once the body dies.

BOOK OF THE DEAD: A collection of texts which first appeared during the New Kingdom and were meant to ensure the deceased's survival in the afterlife.

CANOPIC JARS: Vessels for containing the viscera of the dead. These were under the protection of Horus's four sons: Imsety, Duamutef, Hapy, and Kebehsenuef.

CARTOUCHE: A long, oval band with the first and last names of the pharaoh inscribed on it.

CENOTAPH: An artificial tomb which didn't contain the deceased's body.

CROWNS: Headdresses reserved for gods and kings. There were several: The white crown of Upper Egypt; the red crown of Lower Egypt; the Pshent, the red and white crowns combined to represent a unified Egypt; the blue crown, or Khepresh, which looked like a warrior's helmet; and the Atef crown worn by Osiris, decorated with two feathers.

DROMOS: A road flanked by sphinxes elongating the axis away from a temple for the purpose of aligning it with another edifice or with the Nile.

GOD'S WIFE: The goddess who holds the role of spouse to the god honored in a temple.

HYPOGEUM: A rock-cut tomb.

HYPOSTYLE: A hall whose ceiling is supported by columns.

KA: The element which is equivalent to an individual's personality. It was defined as the preserved vital energy which survived the physical death of the body.

MAMMISI: Edifice where the Egyptians celebrated births of the children of the gods.

MASTABA: An Arabic word meaning "rectangular bench" and used to describe private tombs during the Early Dynastic Period and the Old Kingdom.

NAOS: A word used to describe both the tabernacle in which the statue of a god was placed and the room in which this tabernacle was located. The latter was also referred to as the "holy of holies."

NEMES: A royal head covering comprising two pleated panels hanging from the sides onto the shoulders, and a braided panel hanging from behind.

NOME: A Greek word designating an Ancient Egyptian administrative province.

OSTRACON: A shard of pottery or chip of limestone used as a writing tablet for jotting notes or making drafts.

PSYCHOSTASIA: A word designating the scene in chapter 125 of the Book of the Dead which describes the weighing of the deceased's soul before the grand tribunal of Osiris.

PYLON: Architectural element marking the principal entrance to a temple. It comprises a gateway and two truncated pyramidal towers.

PYRAMID TEXTS: The name given to the texts found on the walls of the sepulchre of Unas (5th Dynasty) and the kings of the 6th Dynasty.

ROYAL TITULARY: The five names taken by a pharaoh upon his ascent to the throne. The chronological order of their apparition is: the Horus name; the two ladies name, Nekhbet and Wadjet; the Golden Horus name; the name of Upper and Lower Egypt; and the Son of Re' name.

SARCOPHAGUS TEXTS: The name given to the texts found on private sarcophagi during the Middle Kingdom. This was the era of the democratisation of the Osiris cult, which guaranteed survival in the afterlife to everyone.

SCEPTER: An attribute carried by the pharaohs and the gods. The scepters were numerous: the was scepter (with a canid head on top) carried by male gods; the wadj scepter (in the form of a papyrus stalk) carried by goddesses; the heqa scepter (a curved baton); and the flagellum of Osiris.

SED FESTIVAL: A royal festival, in theory celebrating 30 years of a monarch's reign.

SEMA TAWY: An Egyptian term meaning "the reunification of the two countries" and a decorative motif symbolizing the union of Upper and Lower Egypt under a single and united kingdom.

SERDAB: A room enclosed in a mastaba and connected to the funerary chapel by a small slit. The serdab contained the statue of the deceased.

SEREKH: A rectangle symbolizing the facade of a palace with a falcon representing Horus on top. The name "Horus" (the pharaoh's first name) was inscribed in it.

SPEOS: A rock-hewn sanctuary.

URAEUS: Term designating the serpent worn by pharaohs and gods on their foreheads or crowns.

USHABTI: A funerary mummiform statuette placed in tombs to do work and daily chores on behalf of the deceased in the afterlife.

BIBLIOGRAPHY

Cyril Aldred,
The Egyptians, Thames and Hudson, London / New York, 1961 / 1984

John Baines et Jaromir Malek,
Atlas of Ancient Egypt, Andromeda, Oxford, 1980 and 1996

Lord Carnarvon and Howard Carter,
Five Years Explorations at Thebes, a record of work done, 1907-1911, Oxford, 1911

Howard Carter,
The tomb of Tutankhamen,
Phyllis J. Walker, 1954

Howard Carter and Arthur Mace,
The tomb of Tut-ankh-amen,
Cassel & Co., London, 1923-1933

Peter A. Clayton,
Chronicle of the Pharaohs,
Thames and Hudson, London, 1994 and 1999

Marc Collier and Bill Manley,
How to read Egyptian hieroglyphs,
British Museum Press, London, 1998 and 1999

Christiane Desroches-Noblecourt,
Toutankhamon, vie et mort d'un pharaon,
Pygmalion, 1988

Raymond O. Faulkner,
The Ancient Egyptian Book of the Dead,
under the management of C. Andrews, London, 1985 and 1996

Raymond O. Faulkner,
The Ancient Egyptian Pyramid Texts (two volumes), Oxford, 1969

Penelope Fox,
Tutankhamun's treasure,
Oxford University Press, London, 1951

Henri Frankfort,
Ancient Egyptian Religion, New York, 1948

Sir Allan Gardiner,
Egypt of the Pharaohs, Oxford / New York, 1961

John Gwyn Griffiths,
The conflict of Horus and Seth from Egyptian and Classical sources,
Liverpool, 1960

John Gwyn Griffiths,
Plutarch's De Iside et Osiride, Swansea, 1970

George Hart,
Egyptian myths, British museum Press

Herodotus,
Histories, Book II, A. B. Lloyd,
Herodotus Book II.1: an intoduction (Leiden, 1975)
Herodotus Book II.2: commentary 1-98 (Leiden, 1976)
Herodotus Book II.2: commentary 99-182 (Leiden, 1988)

Erik Hornung,
Der Eine und die Vielen, Darmstadt, 1971

Claire Lalouette,
Textes sacrés et textes profanes de l'Ancienne Égypte,
Connaissances de l'Orient, Gallimard UNESCO, Paris, 1984

Mark Lehner,
The complete Pyramids, Thames and Hudson, London

Siegfried Morenz,
Osiris und Amun, Kult und Heilige Stätten, Munich, 1966

Georges Posener, Serge Sauneron et Jean Yoyotte,
Dictionnaire de la civilisation égyptienne, Hazan, 1959

Donald B. Redford,
Akhenaten, the heretic king, Princeton, 1995

Nicholas Reeves,
The complete Tutankhamun,
Thames and Hudson, London, 1990

Nicholas Reeves and Richard H. Wilkinson,
The complete Valley of the Kings,
Thames and Hudson, London

Serge Sauneron et Jean Yoyotte,
La naissance du monde selon l'Égypte ancienne,
Sources Orientales I, Seuil, Paris, 1959

Ian Shaw et Paul Nicholson,
British Museum, Dictionary of Ancient Egypt,
British Museum Press, 1995

Jacques Vandier,
Manuel d'archéologie égyptienne,
Éditions A. et J. Picard & Cie, Paris, 1952 à 1964

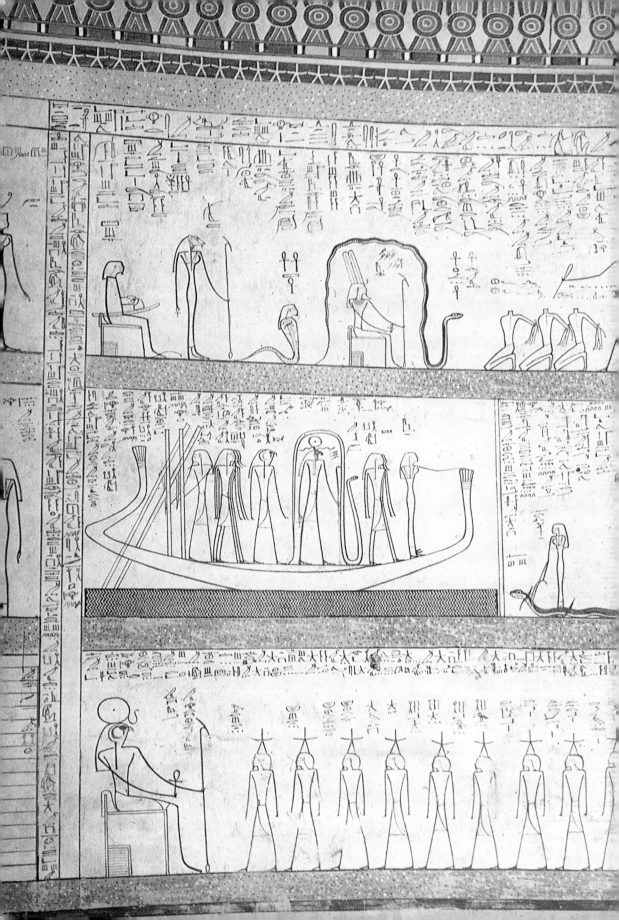